9780517544846

EASY LAWN & GARDEN CARE

 **TEKNOR APEX COMPANY**

• • •

Grateful acknowledgement is made to the following publications for supplying illustrative materials: *Down-To-Earth Vegetable Gardening Know-How, Cash From Square Foot Gardening, Tips for the Lazy Gardener, Feeding the Birds, Roses Love Garlic, The Bug Book, The Joy of Gardening, Growing and Saving Vegetable Seeds,* USDA bulletins, and Country Wisdom bulletins.

Acknowledgement is also made to the following publications for text material used in this book: *Fruits and Berries for the Home Garden, Tips for the Lazy Gardener,* and *Carrots Love Tomatoes.*

Designed by Cindy McFarland

Miscellaneous illustrations by Wanda Harper

Cover photograph by Jerry Pavia.

Thanks to Storey Communications, Inc., whose publications were used throughout as reference and resource materials.

Printed in the United States by Alpine Press
July, 1989

© Copyright 1986 by Storey Communications, Inc.

All rights reserved. No part of this book may be reproduced without permission in writing from the publisher, except by a reviewer who may quote brief passages or reproduce illustrations in a review with appropriate credit; nor may any part of this book be reproduced, stored in a retrieval system, or transmitted in any form by any means — electronic, photocopying, recording, or other — without the written permission of the publisher.

Contents

Chapter		Page
1	Getting Off to a Good Start	1
2	Super Soil	7
3	Creative Landscaping	15
4	Luxurious Lawns	25
5	Gorgeous Flower Gardens	33
6	Bountiful Vegetable Gardens	43
7	Simple Weed and Pest Control	61
8	Easy Maintenance of Trees and Shrubs	75
9	Finishing Touches	83
10	Tips for Continued Success	91

Redemption Coupons

Dear Customer:

Thank you for purchasing your garden hose from the Teknor Apex Company. All of our products are made in the USA to ensure the highest standards in quality and workmanship.

We manufacture a complete line of garden hoses to satisfy the needs of the casual gardener, all the way to the professional and commercial user.

We also manufacture specialty products such as our Soil Soaker™ which is a specially designed leaker hose that uses up to 70% less water! And don't forget our best quality Durafoam brand hoses, which are guaranteed to last a lifetime! And our great Designers' Choice hoses that come in a flowering array of colors.

Whatever your needs, Teknor Apex makes a garden hose for use around the home. Look for our display at a retailer near you.

Thank you,

The Teknor Apex Company

–1–

GETTING OFF TO A GOOD START

How lovely it is to gaze upon a lush, well-tended garden, and an emerald carpet of lawn, trees, and shrubbery pleasantly situated and thriving! Surely you've seen houses—whether in the country, the suburbs, or even in the heart of a city—with just that sort of breath-taking landscape. And perhaps you've even asked yourself: *is this something I could accomplish?*

With a little instruction, the right tools and materials, and the desire, your answer to that question can be a resounding *YES*.

Start at the Beginning

The first step of any undertaking is to evaluate present conditions. Look carefully around your property. Make careful notes in the following categories.

The Lawn

What kind of shape is the lawn in? Is it thick in some spots and bald in others? Is the terrain level or bumpy? Are there steep slopes to be negotiated? Does the soil seem too dry to support a decent turf? Does it become waterlogged after a rain? What about weeds and crabgrass? Write all of this down.

Trees and Shrubs

Are there trees and shrubs on the property? How close to the house? Does it appear as if they were planted by design, or are they simply scattered about? Have they been well-maintained over the years or are they a mass of tangled branches? If you have fruit trees, do they bear well? Do they need pruning? Are there "weed" trees sprouting here and there? Is the shrubbery in need of major trimming and pruning? Once again, make a note of the conditions.

Gardens

Is there a garden site on the property? If yes, is it large enough for your family's needs? Has it been currently worked? Has it been productive? Is the soil on the heavy clay side, or is it sandy? What is the pH or acid level of the soil? Have you had a soil sample from the garden tested for nutrient and organic content? How much sun does the garden get each day? Does the plot slope in any direction? List your answers carefully.

Creating A Plan

As you look over your responses to the questions outlined above, you'll begin to get a pretty good picture of what you have to work with. Transforming your property from what it looks like now to the lush greenery and rich color in your mind's eye may seem like a monumental job. But don't be overwhelmed; your dream can be accomplished a little at a time.

Outline what needs doing in order of its importance to you. For some, it might be the lawn, for others trees and shrubbery captivate the imagination, and for others successful vegetable and flower production will head the list. Often, two or more projects can be started simultaneously. There's a special chapter on each area. One word of caution: don't undertake more than you can realistically handle. You'll become frustrated and the results will show it.

Take your time. Rome wasn't built in a day.

What You'll Need

Nothing is more annoying than not having the right equipment for the tasks at hand. If you're just starting out, investing in a set of quality hand tools is a must. Whenever possible, select tools and implements for their comfort of use. If you're tall, you'll find that long-handled tools will save your back. Consider the weight of tools as well; there's no need to suffer shoulder ache after doing just a little cultivating or digging.

Tools for Lawn and Garden Preparation

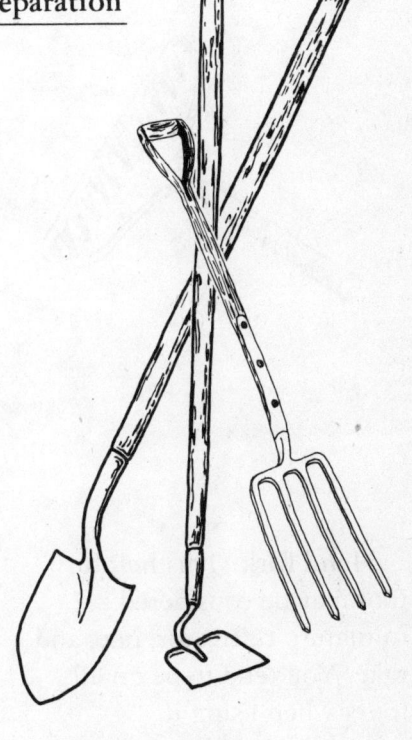

Shovel or spade. Great all-purpose garden tool for digging, spreading, sod-slicing, and stone-prying.

• • •

Spading fork. Another multiple use, indispensable garden tool. Its four heavy-gauge tines make it perfect for breaking sod, aerating soil, digging root crops, turning compost heaps, cleaning out dense animal manure and bedding, and many other tasks. All purpose forks, known commonly as **pitchforks,** have five slender tines for moving lighter loads such as hay and leaves.

• • •

Hoe. This is also a multi-purpose tool used primarily for weeding and cultivating between rows of plants, but heavier versions can be used to dig shallow furrows for planting or irrigation. The narrower the hoe, the better for cultivating between individual plants.

• • •

Cultivator. This implement, which comes in many versions, aerates the soil and chops weeds at the same time. When cultivating close to plants, take care not to damage roots by cultivating too deep.

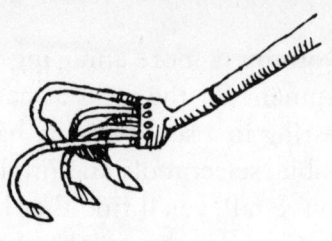

• • •

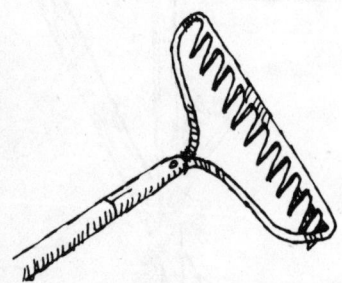

Garden rake. Another garden workhorse, the rake levels and smoothes out seedbeds prior to planting by snagging rocks, roots, and sticks. It's the perfect tool for mixing lime and fertilizer into the upper soil, and for spreading and removing mulches. Also a great surface-scratcher when repairing "bald" spots on lawns.

• • •

Hand fork. This helpful tool may be considered a miniature cultivator, hoe, and rake. You tend to be on all fours when using it.

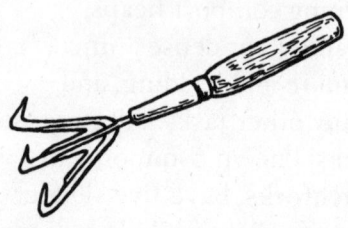

• • •

Hand trowel. This is the indispensable tool for transplanting, and a handy one for applying fertilizer or compost.

4

• • •

Work gloves. No gardener should be without them. They prevent blisters and cuts, and keep you from spending long hours cleaning your fingernails.

Tools for Maintaining Lawns, Trees, and Shrubs

• • •

Grass shears. Perfect for trimming lawns wherever they abut walkways, flower borders, trees, and shrubbery.

• • •

Pruners. A must-have tool for cutting small branches, pruners come in a variety of shapes and weights. Select a pair that feel right in your hand, and come with a good set of grips.

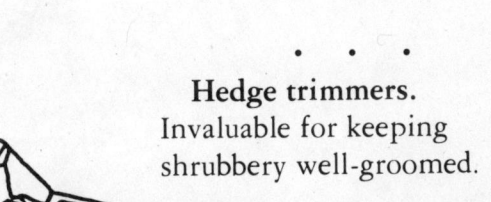

• • •

Hedge trimmers. Invaluable for keeping shrubbery well-groomed.

• • •

Lopping shears. Designed to cut through thick branches, this tool is handy for the home orchardist and those who wish to properly maintain their trees and bushes.

Getting Off to a Good Start 5

Watering Equipment

To be productive, lawns, trees, and gardens must have adequate supplies of water—particularly in areas of low rainfall. There are scores of products and accessories available, ranging from simple garden hoses and sprinklers to sophisticated irrigation and underground sprinkler systems. Here's a sampling of what you're likely to find.

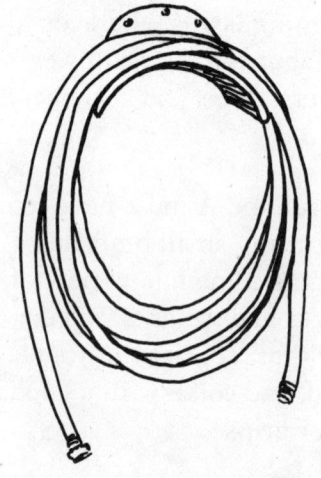

-2-

SUPER SOIL

Rich, healthy soil is the cornerstone of all successful lawns and gardens. Good soil practically guarantees prolific yields, prevents insect and disease attack, and will make your gardens the envy of the neighborhood.

What you may *not* know is that building and maintaining super soil is surprisingly *easy*—once you know how to do it.

First: Test Your Soil

Ideally this should be done in the fall because the test labs are less busy then, and you won't have to wait as long for results. Use a hand trowel to take small amounts of soil from several spots in the garden or lawn at a depth of 6 inches. Mix samples together in a bucket. Allow mixture to dry at room temperature. Put a few ounces in a plastic bag, seal it, and bring it to the nearest Cooperative Extension Service office.

It won't be long before you have a report back indicating the basic nutrient and pH levels in your soil, along with organic content.

Second: Correct the Soil pH

The acidity or alkalinity of the soil (pH level) has a tremendous bearing on how plants and shrubs develop. A pH of 7 is neutral—below that is acid, above is alkaline. Most lawns and gardens thrive between the 5.5 to 7.5 range, with some exceptions.

Your soil report will indicate pH and how it should be adjusted.

To Raise Soil One Unit of pH

100 sq. ft.	Hydrated Lime	Dolomite	Ground Limestone
Light Soil	1½ pounds	2 pounds	2½ pounds
Heavy Soil	3½ pounds	5½ pounds	6 pounds

To Lower Soil One Unit of pH

	Sulphur	Aluminum Sulphate	Iron Sulphate
Light Soil	½ pound	2½ pounds	3 pounds
Heavy Soil	2 pounds	6½ pounds	7½ pounds

Note: The amount of lime you use doesn't have to be as precisely measured as this chart suggests.

Third: Organic Matter Adds Nutrients to the Soil

Whether your soil is dense clay, sievelike sand, or loam, adding organic matter to it regularly (leaves, grass clippings, manure, kitchen waste, etc.) will not only increase the nutrients available to plants, but improve its composition at the same time.

So even if you have the most problematic soil, don't worry—adding organic matter will improve it. Clay, for instance, is composed of tiny flakes that stick together and make the soil difficult to work. When wet, it's mucky; when dry, it's like cement. Sound familiar? Organic matter over time will make even the densest clay soil crumbly and manageable. In sandy soils, organic matter works like a sponge, holding moisture and nutrients until plant roots can get at them.

Ever notice how rich and black the soil is on a forest floor? The reason? Leaves fall, decompose, and replenish the soil with the nourishment to support another season's productive growth. We can take our cue from nature and return to the soil as much as our crops take from it.

Green Manuring

The process of returning to the soil that which is grown with its benefit is called *green manuring*. Specialized cover crops such as rye and buckwheat (also known as green manures) will improve soil quality when turned under. But even turning under crop residues (corn stalks, tomato vines, and thick-rooted crops such as kale) is extremely beneficial. *Leguminous crops*, such as peas and beans, have the ability to take nitrogen—a vital nutrient—from the air and "fix" it in their roots. After you harvest the crop, till or spade the plants under right then and there. What you plant in the vacant space immediately after will benefit immensely.

Compost: The Speedy Natural Fertilizer

The practice of composting is little more than a heating up, and therefore a *speeding up*, of the natural process that takes place on the forest floor. Finished compost, a rich, black, crumbly material, is no more or less than rotted organic matter that has undergone a wonderful transformation in a relatively short amount of time. Here's how to make your own.

Step 1: The Bin

Compost is generally processed in a pile, and for best results, the pile should be contained. The simplest container is a circular wire cage made from about 10 feet of 4-foot-high woven wire fence. If you have large quantities of material to be composted, you may want to make your circular cage larger (each 3 feet of fencing equals approximately 1 foot of diameter), or have several piles going simultaneously.

You can make compost bins from cinder blocks, bales of hay, wooden slats, or even poles. Be guided by your own needs and esthetics. As for location, perhaps the most convenient spot is right in the middle of the garden. But just about any place is fine, so long as you don't have to carry heavy materials too far.

Step 2: Gathering the Materials

Virtually *any* living or once living material is suitable for the compost pile. One steady source is kitchen waste: fruit and vegetable parings, eggshells, spoiled milk, old bread, you name it. Another rich source is leaves, animal manure, weeds from nearby fields that haven't gone to seed yet, grass clippings, and so forth. Some materials such as grass clippings and other fresh nonfibrous materials tend to decompose quicker than others (woody-stemmed plants, sawdust, wood chips, etc.), which explains why a pile of oak leaves or sawdust will sit for years without apparent decay. If the materials available to you fall into the second group, you'll have to add some nitrogen-rich material such as manure, blood meal, or even pulverized dog food to activate the process—use about 2 to 3 pounds for each 100 pounds of the coarser material. Shredding leaves will make them decompose faster. If you don't own a shredder, never fear; your power mower will do the job well enough. Pile up some leaves or other coarse material about 10 inches high. Start up the mower, raise the front wheels, and lower them slowly onto the pile. Rake up whatever gets blown afield and it's ready for the heap.

Step 3: Layering the Materials

Entire books have been written on composting, with particular emphasis on precisely how the materials ought to be layered. One widely accepted system calls for a three-to-one ratio of green matter to manure:

- 6 inches of green matter (grass clippings, weeds, shredded leaves)
- 2 inches of manure or kitchen wastes
- a sprinkling of soil to cover (with an added handful of ground limestone and ground phosphate rock, available in garden stores)

Repeat the layers until the pile is 4 to 5 feet high. Moisten, but don't drown, each layer. Poke holes in the pile to aid aeration. Turn the pile after six weeks, and the compost will be ready to use after another six weeks.

For those of us who aren't that organized, don't worry. Add material when it becomes available. Cover it with soil, keep it moist, and let nature take its course.

Earthworms: The Gardener's Best Friends

Earthworms literally eat their way through the soil, and leave dark castings behind them. These castings are what contribute to soil fertility. One earthworm can produce its weight in castings each day. Clearly then, the more earthworms in the garden, the better.

The number of earthworms in your garden depends directly on how much organic matter there is in your soil. Adding organic matter almost automatically increases the worm population.

If you want to take a worm census, select an area that has a lot of lush growth and dig up a piece of ground that is 1 foot square and about 7 inches deep. Pick through the sample and count the worms. If you find ten, your soil is in good shape. If you find only one or two, it's a sure sign that you need to add more organic matter.

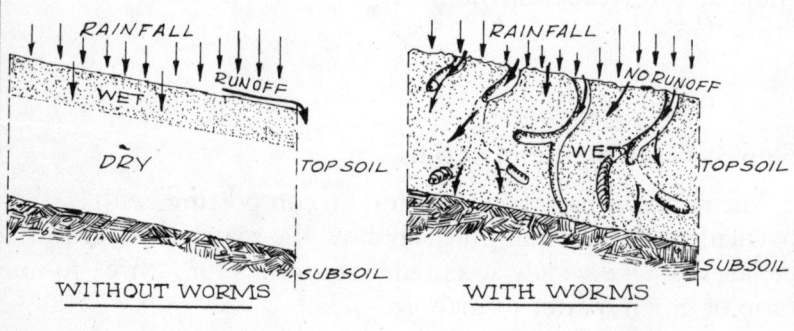

Step 4: The Pile Heats Up

With the proper materials and right amount of air and water, the pile should start heating up in a day or so. If all goes well, the temperature will continue to rise until it stabilizes at about 160°F. Things start to decompose rather quickly now: disease organisms are killed off, weed seeds are burned out, and sometimes the heat build-up

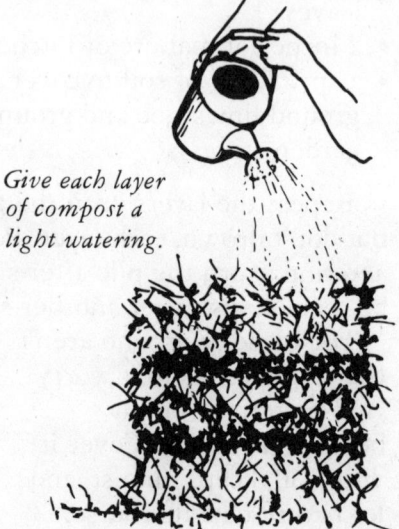

Give each layer of compost a light watering.

will even reduce the microbe population. If that occurs, the pile will cool down until the microbe population can multiply again and the composting process will continue.

Step 5: Turning the Heap

Turning the heap with a spading fork every few weeks lets in air essential to the composting process. It also gets some of the unprocessed materials into the pile's center where the heat is greatest and decomposition fastest.

A well-made compost pile has visible layers.

Step 6: Using the Final Product

If you've made a huge amount of compost, you can spread it over the surface of your garden, and spade or till it under. Or if you have only a limited quantity, use it as a transplanting medium. Dig your transplant holes, fill in the bottom with 3 or 4 inches of compost, add a little plain soil, and set in your plants.

A 5-pound burlap sack of compost suspended in a 20-gallon drum of water or rain barrel will make dandy compost "tea." It is the perfect pick-me-up for watering/sidedressing your plants, and they will love it on those dog days of high summer. Compost sprinkled around the stem of a plant makes a perfect topdressing. Either add water or wait until it rains, and those rich nutrients will filter down through the soil to the thirsty roots below.

Compost Ingredients

This is just a partial list. Some of these items will be easy to find, but others may take a little scavenging. Use your imagination. In the long run, your garden will benefit from your labors.

apple pomace (by-product of cider-making)	kitchen wastes (vegetable and fruit rinds, coffee grounds, etc.)
bird cage cleanings	leather waste and dust
brewery wastes	leaves
buckwheat hulls	manures (cow, horse, rabbit, poultry)
cannery wastes	milk (sour)
evergreen needles	nut shells
chaff	oat hulls
cheese whey	peanut hulls
corn cobs and husks	peat moss
feathers	pond weeds
fish scraps	salt hay
garden residues	sawdust, shredded bark
gelatin-processing waste	seaweed, kelp, eelgrass
grape pomace (by-product of wine-making)	straw
grass clippings	sugar cane
hair	tanbark
	tobacco stems and dust
hay	wood chips

Sheet and Trench Composting

Gardeners who prefer not to wait for a compost heap to do its sometimes slow work can take advantage of an open spot in the garden to do either "sheet" or "trench" composting directly in the soil.

Sheet composting involves spreading organic matter like a sheet over an area and tilling or spading it in immediately. In *trench composting*, you open a pit or furrow, lay in the organic matter, and cover with soil. This works especially well for kitchen wastes that might otherwise start to smell. In each case, the soil microbes and earthworms get right to work. Another advantage of these forms of composting is that no nutrients can leach away as they might in an open bin. And, of course, there's no heavy heap to turn.

–3–

CREATIVE LANDSCAPING

Although most people can recognize and appreciate a beautiful landscape, many cannot imagine creating the beauty themselves. But with a few basic guidelines, proper planning, and a little scheduled upkeep, anyone can turn a colorless plot of land into a dazzling environment.

As with flower and vegetable gardening, home landscaping is an opportunity for personal expression. As long as this idea is kept in mind, *the fun will never stop*. In the end, individual taste and style, *not formal rules*, create the character of the landscape.

Of course, there are practical considerations that bear on every landscape venture:

- the physical assets or liabilities of the land
- the realities of your lifestyle
- your budget

Evaluating the Property

Soil. What is the condition and character of the soil? Does it drain well? Will it support trees and shrubs? Have soil samples taken from different parts of your property tested for organic content, nutrient, and pH levels. See page 7 for instructions, or contact your Cooperative Extension office.

• • •

Climate. Weather conditions govern plant growth, so it would be wise to research the various species appropriate to your local climate. Nurserymen in your area can help to get you on the right track.

• • •

The lay of the land. How your land lies will play a major role in shaping your landscape design. Make a note of all pertinent information:

- Does your land slope or swell, and will that work for or against any early ideas you have about designing the property?
- Are there large outcroppings of stone that create problem barriers, or could they be used to partition space in a desirable way?
- Are there low-lying areas of poor drainage?
- Are there areas where large trees deprive other growth of sun and water?

As you ask yourself these and other questions, consider ways in which you might like to change things. For example, perhaps you want to fill in an existing cavity for a future garden, or level off an embankment that would otherwise create drainage problems. Are such changes affordable? Check with landscape architects or local contractors. Your Cooperative Extension office will be helpful in suggesting some to contact.

• • •

Existing vegetation. You will find it necessary to include in your final plan the trees and shrubs already growing on your land, particularly if they are functional (i.e., they provide shade, windbreaks, partitions). Remember: desired landscaping effects do not happen overnight. Your dreams for a stand of shade trees won't be realized for quite some time after planting, so think twice before eliminating good-sized, existing trees. Besides, a nice mix of older and younger tree and shrub stock creates a certain natural harmony on the land.

Matching Landscape with Lifestyle

Armed now with a sense of what you have to work with, you now can begin to tailor your landscape design to the needs and realities of your lifestyle. Answers to the following questions will help you plan more realistically.

- If you have children, will you want designated play areas?
- How about areas of privacy surrounded by protective hedges?
- Will you want the front of your house to be public, but maintain the backyard area as a secluded retreat? Or would you prefer total privacy?
- Will you want to showcase your house by accenting the foundation with attractive shrubs, or do you prefer a more integrated fabric of architecture, plants, and trees?
- Is there a front road you'll want to block the view of?
- Are there views from existing windows you want to keep or alter?
- Will you want a space for vegetable gardens?
- Do you want to plan for flower beds and borders? Perhaps even a cutting garden?
- Is there a suitable site for a rock garden?
- What about walks, paths, and driveways? Should they retain a natural flavor or do you prefer them to be paved?

Naturally, these are only guidelines. You will likely have dozens more questions and considerations of your own. But make notes of everything—questions and possible answers. You'll need them when you start making sketches of the actual landscape design.

Your Budget

The best budgeting advice you're ever likely to get is: *be realistic*. That doesn't mean you can't have what you want, but it may mean you'll have to wait a while before you can have it all. As a general rule, never underestimate time and money commitments to your landscaping project. Cutting corners is always a good idea, but some shortcuts can wind up costing you more money in the long run. Always feel free to consult landscape architects and nurserymen, even if you are doing the job yourself. They'll be able to provide you with realistic cost estimates for the plan you have in mind. You will have a better idea of what your commitment in time and dollars will be once you have gathered the advice of experts and laid it out for evaluation.

Landscaping on Paper

Generally, landscape designs fall into one of three categories: formal designs, where elements are symmetrically arranged; informal designs, where balance is achieved without symmetry; a combination of formal and informal designs.

Whatever your preference, follow these basic steps for a coherent plan.

1. Measure your lot with a tape measure, or consult your deed for measurements.
2. Draw the lot to scale on a large sheet of graph paper, with each square representing one foot.
3. Enter all existing features on the property: the house, outbuildings, walks and paths, driveway, trees, shrubs, gardens—whatever is already there.
4. Using an erasable pen, enter features you would like to add, keeping in mind the size and shape of the lot and surrounding properties, the location of the house on the lot, its entrances and exits, its traffic patterns. Avoid making the mistake of overplanting. A cluttered lot is rarely attractive and almost impossible to maintain. When choosing trees and plants keep in mind overall effect: consider color, mass, height, cycle of flowering, how certain plantings look in sun and shade, whether plants creep and spread or whether they grow vertically. How will unusual combinations look? How big will certain plantings eventually become? How easy or difficult will they be to maintain?

Okay. Here are some choices for inclusion in your plan.

foundation plantings	rock gardens
shrub borders	perennial borders
hedges	lily pool
ground covers	play area
shade trees	patio or deck
fruit trees	garbage collection area
flower beds	composting area
vegetable gardens	tool shed
new walks and paths	fences

Make several different charts with various planting combinations. It's great fun!

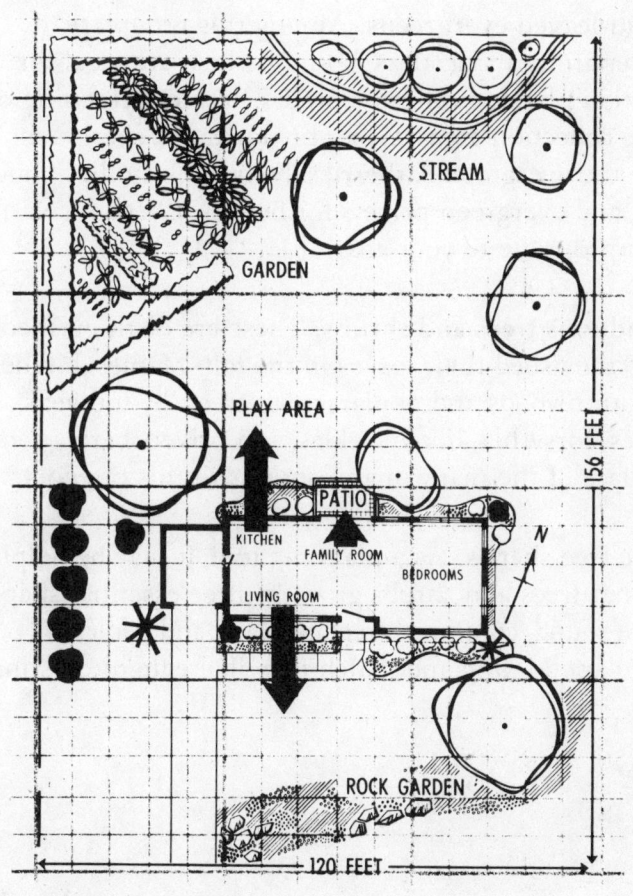

A sample landscape design.

Creative Landscaping 19

Selecting Trees, Hedges, and Shrubs

There are hundreds of varieties of trees and shrubs, but they all fall into three basic groups.

• • •

Conifers. These are needle-leaf or scale-leaf evergreens that produce seed-bearing cones. They include pine, hemlocks, spruces, firs, junipers, and cedars. They are frequently used as windbreaks, along boundary lines, in groves, as hedges, and as foundation plantings. They require little in the way of pruning, but respond well to constant shearing—which is why they're excellent for hedges.

• • •

Broad-leaved evergreens. Among this group are rhododendrons and azaleas, both of which are ideal for foundation plantings, shrub borders, and for screening off garbage collection areas. Other broad-leaved evergreens include the evergreen barberries, boxwoods, hollies, mountain laurels, and evergreen privets for hedges. Check for varieties most appropriate to your area.

• • •

Deciduous trees and shrubs. These are distinguished because they shed their leaves in the fall. Maples, birches, oaks, cottonwoods and poplars, fruit trees, hydrangeas, jasmines, forsythia, honeysuckles, and privets barely scratch the surface of the many, many options in this category.

• • •

Basic tree shapes. As a planning tool, it may be helpful to know that trees and shrubs grow in three essential shapes: they are round, columnar (rectangular), and conical (triangular). Mixing and matching will create interesting variety.

Pin Oak   Lombardy Poplar   Red Cedar   Hemlock

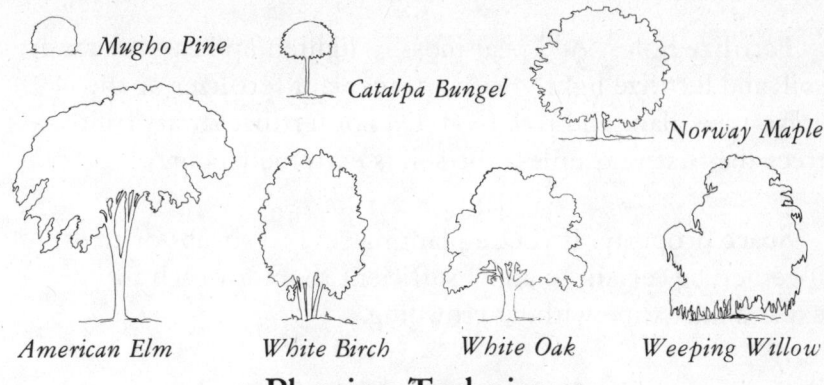

Planting Techniques

Time to plant. Early spring is the best time to plant, but early fall planting is also acceptable.

• • •

Keep roots moist. Whether your trees and shrubs come bare-rooted, planted in containers, or wrapped in burlap, their roots must be kept moist until the actual moment of planting. If there is a delay in planting after you have the trees, place them in a cool cellar or shed, and cover the roots with moist burlap, sawdust or dirt.

• • •

Dig large holes. Holes must accommodate the fanning out of the bare-rooted tree or shrub—usually between 15 and 18 inches in diameter for shrubs, or big enough to accommodate the entire root ball for trees.

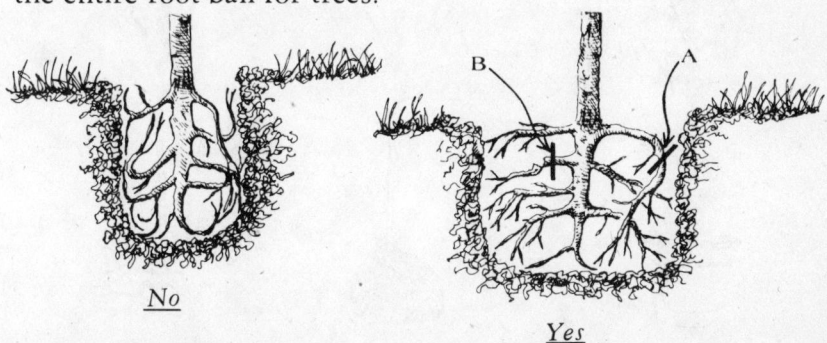

Dig a hole big enough to allow the roots to spread naturally. Very long roots should be pruned to prevent curling under (A). Roots that are broken should be cut off to the break (B).

Creative Landscaping   21

* * *

Fertilize holes. Add peat moss to lighten up heavy or sandy soil, and fertilize lightly with a transplant fertilizer or the spike-type plant and tree food. Do not fertilize dwarf fruit trees the first year unless the soil is extremely poor.

* * *

Space properly. If you're planting several shrubs or trees together, be certain to allow sufficient room for each to expand over time without crowding.

* * *

Set trees or shrubs in. Set in *bare-rooted stock* as illustrated above. Cut off broken roots, trim those that are excessively long. Fill in the hole with soil, making sure not to cover the bud union—the bulge at the base of the trunk. For *canned* shrubs or trees, remove the containers carefully, and set in the hole so that the soil around the roots is at the same level as the surrounding soil or lawn. For *balled and burlapped* stock, there's no need to remove the burlap—it will soon disintegrate. Cover as above, and tamp soil to squeeze out air pockets.

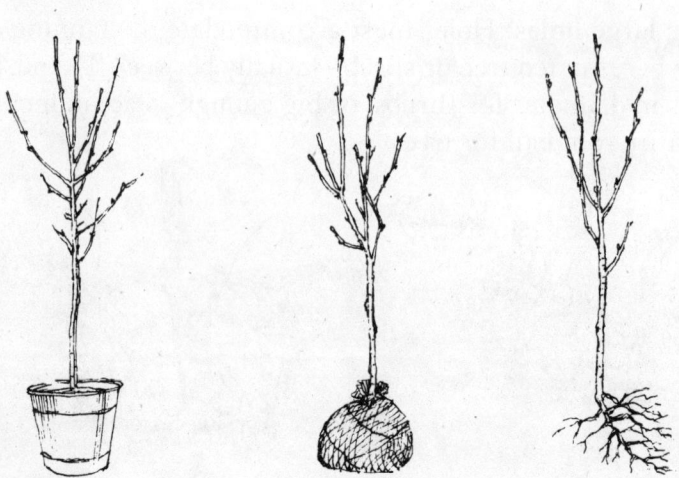

New and young trees are available (from left) in cans or containers, balled and burlapped, or bare-rooted. Bare-rooted trees should be pruned back (right) to restore balance.

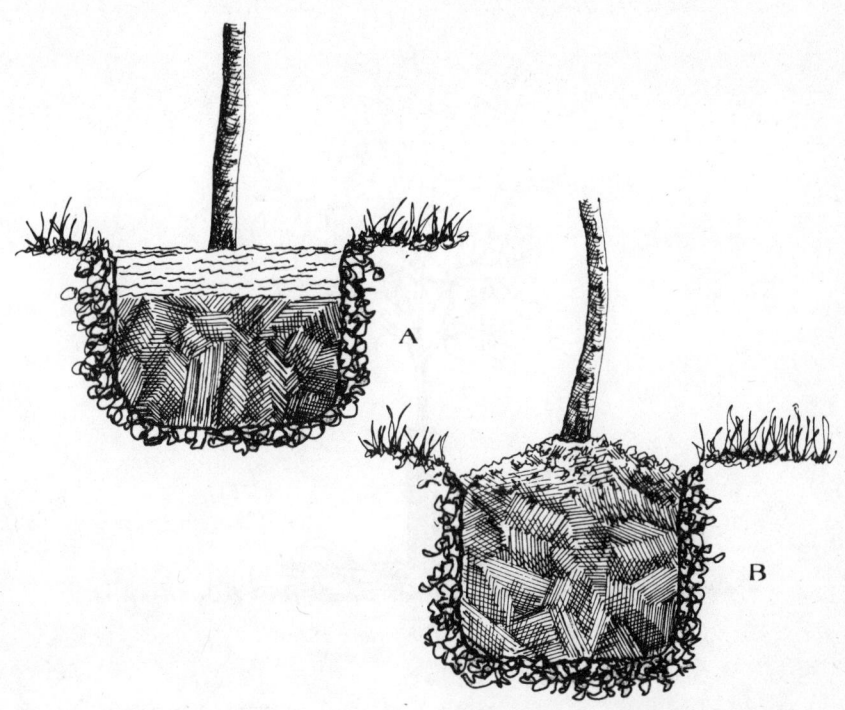

After you have set the new trees in the hole, fill it up with a thick layer of soil and then a fair amount of water (A). Once the water has soaked in, fill the hole with more soil — over and above the level of the ground (B).

• • •

Make a circular watering trench. With your hand or a small trowel dig a shallow trench around the outer circumference of the planting holes. Fill and refill the trench with water until the tree or shrub roots are thoroughly soaked. Water regularly over the first few months to prevent roots from drying out.

• • •

Staking. Occasionally, trees come from the nursery already staked. More often, however, you'll have to stake newly planted trees to keep them straight. Set sturdy wood stakes close to the young tree and attach with strong twine. Ties should be loose around the new tree to allow for trunk growth and to prevent girdling. For young trees with stout trunks about 3 inches in diameter, try guy wires.

Trunk guard for young trees.

• • •

Protect tender trunks. Rabbits, mice, and deer will nibble on the tender bark of young trees. The result can be fatal for the saplings. Special wrappings that discourage such marauding are available at garden centers.

For further details on maintaining trees and shrubs, see chapter 8.

–4–

LUXURIOUS LAWNS

Lush green carpets of lawn are gorgeous to look at, but they don't get that way all by themselves. Keeping a lawn in tip-top shape, free of disease, and largely free of insect pests, involves regular care. Mowing twice a week in the height of the growing season may seem like a lot of work, but when the job's done and you gaze over your handiwork, not much can compare with the sense of pride and accomplishment you'll experience.

Lawn maintenance falls into several categories: watering, mowing and raking, fertilizing, liming, renovation, and weed and pest control. Let's look at them one at a time.

Watering

A newly-built lawn, or a section of lawn just repaired, should be lightly watered until grass seed germinates. After germination, water less frequently but more deeply. Lawns should receive 1 inch of water per week under normal conditions, and 2 inches during dry spells, but never so much that the lawn becomes waterlogged. Whether you use a hose or a sprinkler be sure that water is distributed to your entire lawn evenly.

Mowing and Raking

Mow off dead grass first thing in spring, and thoroughly

rake up leaves and other organic debris which may cover the soil and prevent proper aeration and water uptake by grass roots.

When mowing a newly-established lawn or section of lawn, be certain the mower blade is sharp or it will pull up young seedlings. When the grass has grown to 1½ inches, cut it back to an inch. Cut the grass to 1-inch height two or three more times, and then maintain the lawn at 2 inches. In areas of winter snowfall, let grass grow to 3 inches late in the season.

Mow older lawns twice a week during periods of rapid growth. If the turf is thin, let the clippings stay where they fall, but rake clippings from a thick turf or the grass may burn out under the clippings and die.

Fertilizing

For most lawn grasses, spread about 10 pounds of turf grade fertilizer per 1,000 square feet of lawn at the start of the growing season. Increase this amount to between 30 and 40 pounds during the height of the growing season, but reduce to 15 pounds toward the end of the season. Many popular lawn fertilizers are combined with herbicides and insecticides for weed, crabgrass, and pest control. If you have a problem with unwanted weeds or serious insect infestations, consider using these products. Water thoroughly immediately after application.

Liming

By liming the soil you change its chemical nature. Not only is it made less acid, but other minerals in the soil are altered to forms that make better plant food, and some harmful elements in the soil are rendered powerless. Lime also improves soil texture because clay is broken up and sand compacted, and it aids the process by which soil bacteria put valuable nitrogen in plant-food form.

The results of your soil test will indicate whether your lawn needs lime. Liming makes the soil less acid, so if the pH is less than 7, lime can bring it up to a more beneficial pH measure. But it would probably be a good idea to spread lime over a limited turf area and watch for results. You may find that some lawns respond to lime better than others.

Liming can be done any time of year, but preferably at either end of the season. A soil test will determine specific quantities to apply. A rule of thumb in slightly more acidic soils is to spread between 50 and 80 pounds per 1,000 square feet of lawn once every two to three years. If you've just spread fertilizer, wait until it has washed into the soil before applying lime.

Renovation

Occasionally, and for a variety of reasons, grass may fail to grow here and there. Or perhaps you have decided to tear up a section of lawn overrun by crabgrass. These bare spots are unsightly and should be promptly reseeded. Here are the steps you should follow.

Step 1. Remove all unwanted weeds and debris from the area to be seeded over.

Step 2. Scratch or "slice" the soil with a rake or cultivator.

Step 3. Sprinkle seed, using only superior varieties.

Step 4. Spread a dusting of fertilizer that contains a preemergence weed killer and tamp or roll lightly in place.

Step 5. Water immediately, and keep it coming until seed has germinated and new plants are well-established.

Step 6. Mow when grass plants are 2 inches tall.

Controlling Lawn Thatch

Thatch is a layer of partially decomposed leaves, stems, and roots on the surface of the soil. Some grasses build up thatch more quickly than others. Thatch limits good lawn growth by keeping air, water, and fertilizer from reaching the grass roots. It can heat up under the right conditions and create brown spots all over the lawn. Thatch can also harbor disease organisms.

To determine if you have an unhealthy thatch buildup on your lawn, cut out small plugs from several locations. If thatch is there, you'll recognize it as a spongy layer of material just above the soil.

Dethatching machines can be rented to remove thatch. Or you can buy a dethatching attachment for your rotary mower. Another option, if you have the energy, is to remove thatch by raking vigorously with a metal leaf rake. Gather up the debris and toss it on the compost.

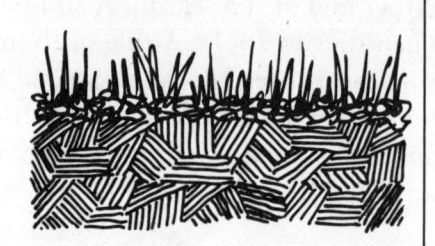

Lawn with a layer of harmful thatch.

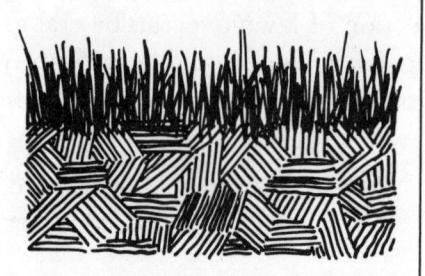

Healthy lawn.

Weed and Pest Control

Getting Rid of Weeds

There are five basic types of lawn weeds, some easier to deal with than others.

• • •

Annual broadleaf weeds. Included in this group are pigweed, ragweed, mustard, and lambsquarters. Mowing usually keeps them well under control.

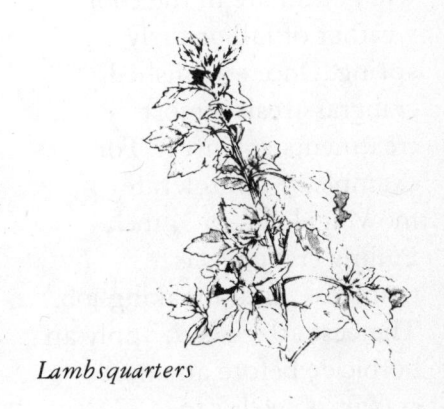

Lambsquarters

• • •

Broadleaf perennials. Broadleaf perennials and biennials include dandelions, chicory, dock, plantain, thistles, and sorrel. They can be controlled chemically or by hand pulling.

• • •

Creeping weeds. Small, creeping weeds such as chickweed, knotweed, ground ivy, and clover manage to find their way into even the best-kept lawns. Controlling these weeds by hand is almost impossible, and they are not entirely responsive to chemical herbicides either. Spot treatment seems to be the method of choice for most gardeners.

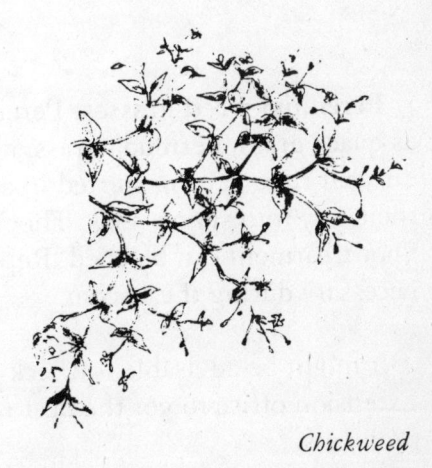

Chickweed

Luxurious Lawns 29

Annual weed grasses. Annual grasses such as crabgrass, goosegrass, and foxtails tend to find their way into lawns that are sparse. Each year these grasses produce millions of seeds that will germinate in the cool weather of fall or early spring. Once established, crabgrass resists most treatments against it. For example, it can tolerate mowing down to ¼ inch. Pulling crabgrass is a thankless, back-breaking job. The best attack is to apply an herbicide before anymore crabgrass seeds can germinate. But there are postemergence chemical treatments available as well.

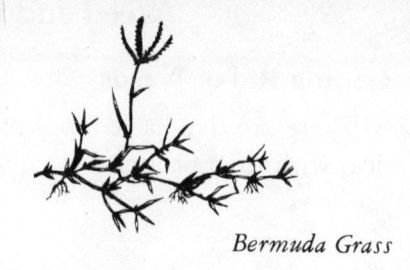

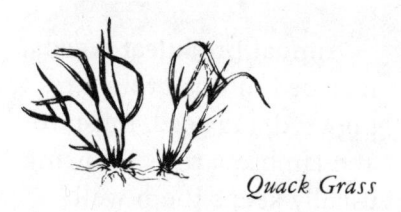

Bermuda Grass

Quack Grass

Nut Grass

Bindweed

Perennial weed grasses. Perennial or hay-type grasses such as quack grass, Bermuda grass, nut grass, and bindweed have a difficult time getting started in a tight turf, but seem to find their way into sparse sods. They're quite difficult to control. Spot treatment can be tried. Repeat applications will be necessary during the season.

It might be advisable to check with your local Cooperative Extension office to get the best remedies for local weed problems.

Getting Rid of Insect Pests

Lawn pests fall into four categories:

• • •

Insects that infest soil and roots. Grubs, ants, mole crickets, wireworms, cicada-killer wasps, wild bees, periodical cicadas, billbugs, and earthworms. Grubs are the most troublesome of lawn pests. They are the larvae of insects such as Japanese beetles, different species of chafers, armyworms, and June bugs, to name only a few. The adults lay eggs in the lawn, which hatch out into an army of hungry grubs that feed on grass roots. The result: dead grass plants, and brown, lifeless areas in your lawn. Tunneling and burrowing ants can also be a problem. Diazinon, Carbaryl, and Dursban (trade name) are effective controls against these insects.

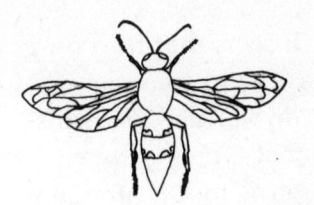

Cicada-Killer Wasp

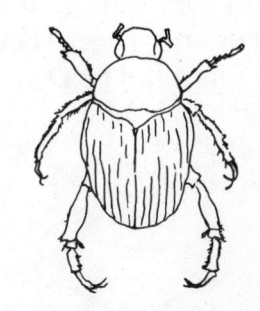

Japanese Beetle

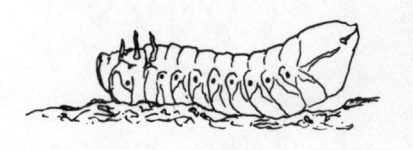

Green June Beetle Grub

Sod Webworm

Sod Webworm (adult)

Luxurious Lawns 31

• • •
Insects that feed on grass leaves and stems. Armyworms, cutworms, billbugs, fiery skipper, Lucerne moths, grasshoppers, leaf bugs, fruit flies. Many of the insects in this group do most of their damage at the larval or grub stage. They are easily controlled by Diazinon, Carbaryl, and Dursban.

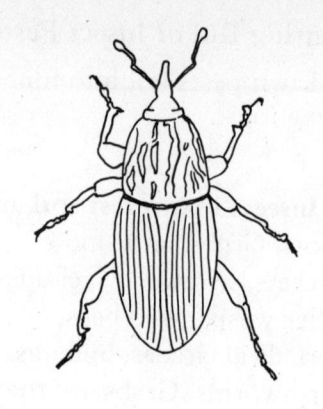

Billbug

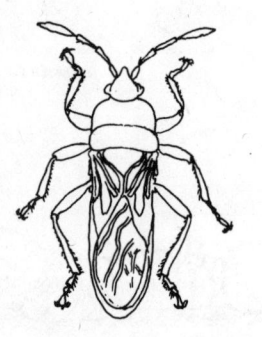

Chinch Bug (winged adult)

• • •
Insects that suck plant juice. Chinch bugs, false chinch bugs, scale insects, leafhoppers, mites, and spitlebugs. Diazinon is an effective control against many of these.

• • •
Insects that inhabit but don't damage lawns. Earwigs, ticks, chiggers, thrips, slugs and snails, millipedes and centipedes, spiders and scorpions, and fleas. Only serious infestations should be dealt with, but if you're spraying and dusting against pests in the other groups, it is likely that the insects in this group will be controlled simultaneously.

When using sprays and dusts, use care and follow directions exactly for controlling specific pests. It is also a good idea to check with the Cooperative Extension office to obtain specific recommendations for treating local lawn troublemakers.

–5–

GORGEOUS FLOWER GARDENS

Have you ever seen those fabulous fireworks that erupt and explode in endless showers and waves of color that never seem to end? Well-planned flower borders, beds, and gardens may not have the thunder of a fireworks display, but when designed with a sense of color and a little timing know-how, they're every bit as breathtaking.

As you will see below, there are many kinds of flowering plants. Some have a lifetime of only one season, but others, with care, may last for generations. The focus of this chapter is on the one-season varieties. They're simple to plant, and require only minimal care to produce dazzling blooms all season long. Perhaps best of all—you can try new ones every year!*

A familiarity with the most common flower gardening phrases will go a long way toward eliminating confusion.

Annuals

There is an enormous variety of these flowers, which complete their life cycle in a single season. They sprout, flower, make seeds, and die between spring and winter. Annual flowers are noted for their brilliant colors—nature's way of attracting pollinating insects. Once they start to flower,

---

*If you are interested in perennial flowers, excellent sources to consult are the *Time-Life Book of Perennials* and *Crockett's Flower Garden*.

most annuals continue to produce blooms for the entire season.

Biennials

These plants require two seasons to produce flowers and then seeds, after which they, too, die. It is possible to start biennials early enough in the growing season to induce them to flower in their first season.

Perennials

These flowers can take two years to come to bloom, although with a long growing season—or if started indoors from seed—they have little trouble flowering in their first year. Once established, they will bloom for specific periods each summer—often as long as a month. Perennials should never be allowed to produce seed because it weakens the plants. Propagation is usually done by root/clump division of the plants after they become mature.

Flower beds and borders. These colorful and decorative narrow bands are usually located on either side of a walk or driveway, at the edges of lawns, and alongside buildings. *Island beds* are set out in the open where they can be seen from all sides. Borders are generally planted against foundation walls or property-line fences, or in front of a hedge. Borders should never be so wide that you must step into them to cultivate.

• • •

Cutting gardens. Designed to grow blooms for harvest and indoor use, cutting gardens are planted in straight rows much like vegetables to simplify cutting. A cutting garden eliminates the need to cut blooms from, and thereby deplete, your flower borders.

• • •

Nursery beds. These are generally small, out-of-the-way plots used for starting perennial or annual seedlings. Here flowers are free to come to full size before they are transplanted to another location.

Choosing the Right Location

Locating flower beds, borders, and gardens is a task that combines esthetics and practicality. Here are some things to consider before you pull out the trowel and cultivator.

• • •

Exposure. How much sun does the prospective site receive each day? If your heart is set on establishing a flower border in an area that doesn't receive much sunlight, don't despair. There are many varieties that not only tolerate shade but thrive in it. However, most annuals and perennials do best in full or at least half sun.

• • •

Soil. Although flowers grown in a rich soil will do better than flowers in a nutrient-poor medium, flowers don't as a rule demand that the soil be especially fertile in order to produce abundant blooms. In fact, some annuals, such as nasturtiums, flower best in poor soil. Check your seed catalog for information on specific varieties. If the spot you've chosen has poor soil though, it might be wise to add some organic matter before planting (see chapter 2).

• • •

Drainage. Like vegetables, most flowers don't like sitting around in water. But even an area with poor drainage can be improved almost immediately by adding quantities of builder's sand, peat moss, and other organic material.

• • •

Views from windows. Part of the fun of having beautifully landscaped property is being able to see it—even from inside. Many flower gardeners plant their beds and borders where they are visible from frequently looked-out-of windows.

• • •

Access to house. You don't want to walk too far to find your flowers either.

Planning Your Flower Garden

Once you involve yourself with flower gardening, you'll hear a great deal about the way things *ought* to be done. Let flexibility reign: beauty and pleasure are the goals. Feel free to experiment, trying combinations that appeal to you.

However, there are some organizing guidelines to keep in mind when sketching your borders and beds on paper. With your seed catalogs open in front of you, there are a number of things you should consider first.

Height of Plants

Flowering plants can range in height from 3 or 4 inches, to several feet tall. Beds and borders traditionally consist of plants of varying heights, with the tallest plants placed at the rear of the border, so they don't block the shorter plants from view. In an island bed, the tallest plants are located in the center and the shorter ones taper off toward the far edges.

Color of Plants

The flower garden can be a personal expression of creativity. There are no rules, especially when it comes to selecting colors. However, to help visualize the effect you hope to create, try using brightly colored magic markers in your sketching. See what beds of a single color look like; then try marking in some contrasts. Keep a lot of paper on hand!

Blooming Times

Another important variable in planning a flower garden is knowing when the plants you've chosen will begin to flower, and how long the blooms are likely to keep coming. The obvious goal is to have at least some color all of the time. Bloom time can be extended if you are religious about removing spent blooms.

Shape, Texture, Foliage

The actual appearance of various plants will influence individual preferences. Some gardeners tend to choose plants with a similar "look," but others may prefer combining many textures and shapes. Consider variety in leaf color and texture as well as in flower color.

Preparing the Seedbeds

Preparing the soil for planting flowers is virtually identical to the procedure for starting a vegetable patch (see page 52). A nice touch is to raise the planting bed slightly above adjacent surfaces of lawns and walks to "show off" the flowers more prominently. When a border planting is made against a solid background, the soil is generally higher in the rear and slopes gently toward the front—for more dramatic display and improved drainage. As for soil fertility, a less rich medium may yield more flowers: marigolds planted as companions in rich vegetable beds often produce more leaf than blooms.

Planting

Direct seeding or transplanting? Although most quick-growing annuals can be seeded directly in the garden once the soil is warm enough, the trend in annual flower gardening is to start with *transplants*—either those you buy at the local garden center or those you grow from seed indoors. In any case, to simplify planting, many seed companies have developed *seed tapes* and *pelleted seeds* for easy handling. See pages 55 to 58 for details on indoor seeding and plant care. If you only have a limited amount of space indoors to start flower seedlings, don't worry. Whatever you can't grow inside you can buy.

You do not need to dig very deeply to set your annuals in the ground because their roots are shallow. For most annuals, cultivation of the soil to a depth of 1 foot is sufficient, or note the depth suggested on the seed package.

Plant Selection

Popular Annuals

The species below are relatively easy to grow from seed outdoors anywhere in the United States.

Alyssum	Impatiens
Amaranthus	Marigold
Aster	Nasturtium
Bachelor Button	Nicotiana
California Poppy	Sunflowers
Candytuft	Sweet William & Pinks
Cosmos	Tithonia
Dahlia	Verbena
Gloriosa daisy	Zinnia

Below are three species that *love to climb*. Plant them near a trellis, a tree stump, fences, wooden lattice, or rig up a piece of string or twine that the plant will climb.

Morning Glory
Scarlet Star Glory
Crimson Star Glory

The following species will make lovely *dried flowers* after you have enjoyed their blossoms for a short time in the garden.

Feathertop   Globe Amaranth   Statice
Fountain Grass   Strawflowers

Best for Beds and Borders

The plants listed here have long-lasting and colorful blooms, and are generally available from nurseries and garden centers.

Begonia, Wax
Celosia
Chrysanthemum
Coleus
Dahlia
Dusty miller
Geranium
Gloriosa daisy
Impatiens

Marigold
Nasturtium
Nicotiana
Pansy
Petunia
Snapdragon
Salvia
Verbena
Zinnia

If you are faithful about picking your pansies, they will keep on blooming.

Best Edging Plants

These are popular, low-growing bedding plants that look especially good in front of tall flowers. Many are compact, though others spread a bit as they mature. Check seed catalog for proper spacing.

Ageratum
Alyssum
Aster, dwarf
Begonia, dwarf
Browallia, dwarf
Candytuft
Dianthus
Dusty miller
Forget-me-not

Impatiens, dwarf
Lobelia
Marigold, dwarf
Pansy
Petunia
Phlox, dwarf
Portulaca
Snapdragon, miniature
Zinnia, miniature

Best Annuals for Shady Growing

What follows is a list of flowers that do well in a broad range of shady conditions. The seed packet or catalog will tell you exactly how much shade and water the plant will tolerate, and you can plan accordingly.

Begonia
Browallia

Coleus
Impatiens

Lobelia
Forget-me-not

Primula
Salvia splendens

Gorgeous Flower Gardens

Roses

No section on flower gardening would be complete without at least some mention of these exotic blooms. There are essentially six types of roses available for home growing. You can buy quality rose bushes from a reputable nurseryman or through a mail-order garden catalogue. Both of these sources will provide you with instructions on proper care and maintenance.

Hybrid tea roses are those which most closely resemble commercial roses. They grow on bushes that range in height from 2 to 6 feet, are available in many colors, and are perhaps the most popular of all roses. In warm climates plant them 3 feet apart, otherwise 2 feet.

Floribunda roses grow in clusters on short stems, and are more for show outdoors than for cutting. Planting distance depends on type.

Grandiflora roses are a cross between hybrid teas and floribundas: the blooms grow in bunches, but on long stems for convenient cutting. Some bushes grow quite large. Plant 2 to 3 feet apart, depending on variety.

Tree roses are roses grafted onto special root stock that grows to a height of 5 or 6 feet. Hybrid teas, floribundas, grandifloras, and miniature roses are among the types that can be grafted to special stock. They are *not* easy to grow, and are quite costly. Check with a nurseryman for planting distances.

Climbing roses can grow up to 20 feet in height, must be supported on trellises, and come in several varieties. Some produce blooms all summer, though others flower in mid-spring and again in the fall. Plant 8 to 16 feet apart, depending on variety.

Miniature roses produce blooms in a wide range of beautiful colors, but generally only reach a height of 8 to 10 inches. There are climbing varieties available, along with miniature tree stock that rarely exceeds 1 foot in height.

• • •

Planting note. Roses love full sun, but will produce blooms in a spot that receives only partial sun. If you have a choice, morning sun is best. Also, if you only have access to one side of your rose bed, keep it less than two feet wide. If access is from both sides, the bed can be a foot wider.

Flowering Bulbs Light Up the Spring

It is a delight to see the first greenery of spring emerge—ready to burst into color! And what you're looking for from flowering bulbs is a big display, so always plant bulbs in clumps and patches, never individually.

Hardy bulbs are planted in the fall to produce flowers the following spring. They can withstand even severe freezing. Set them in rich, well-drained soil using the same hand tools (trowel, cultivator) that you will use in the vegetable garden. Be sure you plant bulbs at the depth appropriate to the species—check the seed catalogue, a good reference book, or consult an employee at your local garden center. If your soil is poor, add well-rotted or composted manure, but never fresh manure, because it can burn tender roots as they begin to sprout. Bone meal is also very beneficial to bulbs. By all means plant the most popular types, but you may want to try some of the lesser known but equally beautiful types as well. Here's a partial listing:

Crocus	Grape Hyacinth	Lily
Daffodil	Hyacinth	Snowdrop
Dutch Iris	Iris	Tulip
Freesia	Jonquil	Windflower

Tender bulbs are intolerant to freezing, so they must be dug up in areas where the ground freezes and replanted in spring. Some popular tender bulbs are *Caladium, Canna, Dahlia, Gladiolus*, and *Tuberous begonia*.

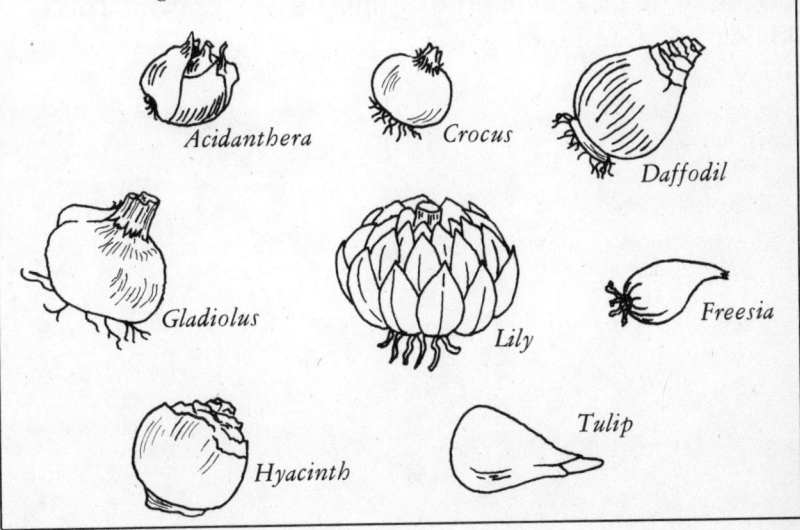

Acidanthera

Crocus

Daffodil

Gladiolus

Lily

Freesia

Hyacinth

Tulip

Gorgeous Flower Gardens

Caring for Growing Flowers

Thin, thin, thin! If you have directly seeded your flower plants in the garden, make sure they are not overcrowded. Thin plants to the desired spacing.

• • •

Weed, weed, weed! Keep all flower beds free from weeds. Once the ground has warmed up, mulch heavily with leaves, straw, sawdust, wood chips, pine needles, and such. This will smother most weeds.

• • •

Water, water, water! Keep the water coming, especially during dry periods.

• • •

Pinch back. To increase the number of flowers a plant bears, pinch off the tip of the stem *above* the topmost leaves. This pinching back is done when a young plant is 2 to 4 inches tall and has three or four sets of leaves. A plant whose tip has been pinched back will be bushier and produce a number of flowering branches.

• • •

Harvest regularly. Cutting will stimulate many annuals to produce more blooms, so harvest often. When blossoms fade on the stem, pick them off to stimulate new growth. This is known as "dead-heading."

–6–

BOUNTIFUL VEGETABLE GARDENS

Little else in life provides as much pleasure as one's own patch of healthy vegetables. For one thing, a vegetable garden is a thing of beauty. For another, gardening is a satisfying hobby—all the more so when one considers the health benefits. Anyone can garden. Starting off on the right foot will help guarantee success.

Choosing the Right Site

When selecting a site to locate your garden, several factors should be kept in mind.

Exposure. The ideal garden spot should be exposed to abundant sunshine for much of the day—at least six hours' worth.

• • •

Slope. Slope can have a bearing on gardening success. Just a few degrees of pitch to the south or west exposes soil to more direct rays from the sun, allows the garden to warm up earlier in the year, and lets you start planting sooner. Too much slope—anything more than a ten-degree tilt—may create erosion problems, and make it uncomfortable to work.

• • •

Look for lush growth. If there's a spot on your property that grows the thickest lawn, or the healthiest-looking stand of weeds, that's probably the best place to locate your garden.

• • •

Avoid trees and shrubs. Whenever possible, keep your garden away from tall trees and shrubs. Their far-reaching roots will creep into the garden and steal away precious nutrients and water from your vegetable crops.

• • •

Check for good drainage. Most vegetables don't do well in soil that is wet and soggy most of the time. Avoid low-lying areas with poor drainage; establish your garden on higher ground whenever possible.

Choosing the Right Time

There are many climate variations in the United States. Even in southern states there are distinct zones, and gardeners would do well to time the planting of their cool and warm weather vegetable crops accordingly.

Below you will find a chart that gives you a rough idea of when to plant your warm and cool weather crops according to your location.

	Cool Weather Crops	Warm Weather Crops
North	March—June August—September	May—June
South	February—April August—September	March—July
Gulf Coast/ Southwest	September—February	March—April
Tropical Florida	September—February	November—February
Coastal California	February—April August—October	April—June

These are approximate recommendations. The seed packet, and your knowledge of the area, should provide you with the best guidelines for when to plant your crops to enjoy maximum yield, and avoid damage from frost or heat.

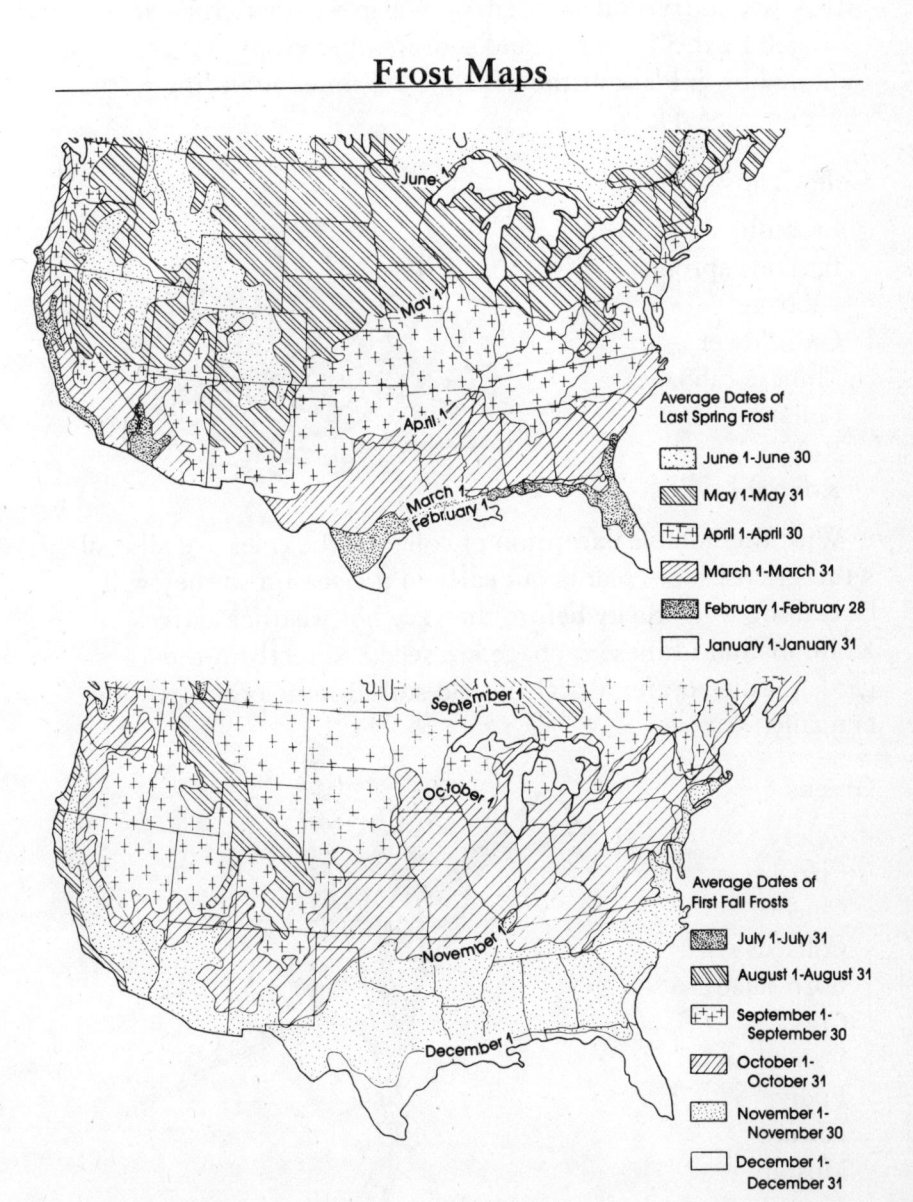

Frost Maps

Average Dates of Last Spring Frost
- June 1-June 30
- May 1-May 31
- April 1-April 30
- March 1-March 31
- February 1-February 28
- January 1-January 31

Average Dates of First Fall Frosts
- July 1-July 31
- August 1-August 31
- September 1-September 30
- October 1-October 31
- November 1-November 30
- December 1-December 31

Time your planting according to these charts to avoid damage and loss from killing frosts.

Bountiful Vegetable Gardens 45

Choosing the Vegetables

There are several groups of related vegetables from which to make your choices. It's fun to experiment; leave yourself a little space to try something new. Warm weather crops are indicated by the ‡ symbol, and cool weather crops are indicated by §. Plant at the appropriate times according to the chart on page 44.

Cole Crops §

   Broccoli
   Brussels sprouts
   Cabbage
   Cauliflower
   Chinese cabbage
   Collards
   Kale
   Kohlrabi

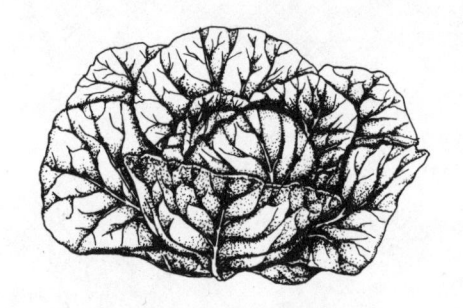

With the notable exception of collards, the coles are all cool weather crops. Set plants out early in the season so they will be coming to maturity before the very hot weather arrives. Kohlrabi and Chinese cabbage are seeded directly in the garden. Coles prefer a slightly acid soil. Rotate locations annually.

Greens §

   Celery
   Chard
   Chicory
   Collards
   Corn salad
   Cress
   Dandelion
   Endive
   Lettuce
   Mustard
   New Zealand spinach
   Spinach

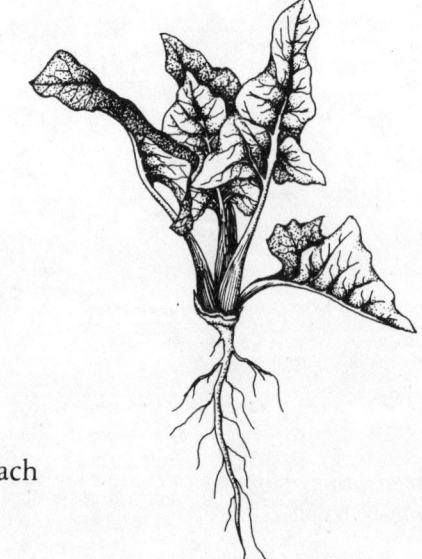

Greens cover a multitude of plant families, but all make for great eating and a wonderful variety of color and texture in the garden. Although chard, collards, and New Zealand spinach can tolerate summer heat, the great majority of greens do best in the cool weather at either end of the growing season. Keep greens well-watered and fed, and if possible, place them in a section of the garden that gets some shade. They'll thank you with bountiful harvests of sweet, crisp salads for much of the season.

Onion Family §

Garlic
Leeks
Onions
Shallots

Though onions can be grown from seed, it takes a lengthy growing season to get them to maturity. The most popular method of planting onions is with sets, or immature bulbs. They make rapid growth, and you can pull them for scallions as soon as they've reached 8 to 10 inches of top growth. Garlic and shallots—essential for gourmet cooking—are also planted from sets. The best way to raise leeks is from plants started indoors or purchased from a nursery. All onion family members require good, rich soil for optimum production.

Beans ‡

Dry beans
Green beans
Shell beans
Soy beans

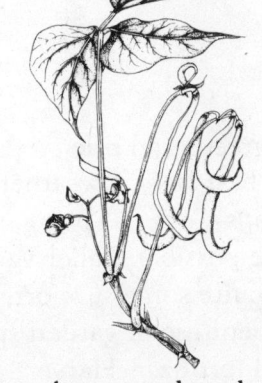

Every garden should have at least one variety of beans. The most popular are green or *snap* beans that are grown for their edible pods. There are *bush* varieties that grow fairly low to the ground, and there are *pole* beans which must be trained onto vertical supports.

Bountiful Vegetable Gardens

Shell beans include the limas, southern or "black-eyed" peas, and horticultural beans, grown for the soft beans within the inedible pods, and *dry* beans (Red Kidney, French Horticultural) are taken from plants which have been allowed to mature and dry. The hard, dry seeds are then separated from their pods (threshed) and stored for use in soups, stews, and the like.

Tomatoes and Other Nightshades ‡

Eggplant   Potato
Peppers   Tomato

Tomatoes are the most popular garden crop in America. They come in many sizes and colors, and are easy to grow provided they are given adequate sunshine, nutrients, and water. Larger types may require support or can be allowed to sprawl over dry mulch. Use disease-resistant varieties whenever possible. In extremely hot weather, harvest tomatoes when they are pink and allow them to ripen indoors. Eggplant and potatoes require extremely fertile conditions, though peppers must be only modestly fertilized. All demand a steady water supply. Potatoes and eggplant may be harvested quite young; peppers should be picked when they have reached full size. Ripe peppers are red, but can be harvested and eaten green.

Peas ‡

Like greens and cole crops, peas do best in cool weather. Two crops—one in spring, the other timed to mature in the fall—are possible. Taller varieties, including edible podded peas, require some support. Try growing peas in wide rows for efficient use of garden space. Peas require little in the way of added fertilizer. Harvest peas when pods have filled out, but don't let them get too large or they'll have lost their sweetness.

Root Crops §

Beets
Carrots
Parsnips
Radishes
Rutabagas
Turnips

Root crops are relatively easy to grow, but can be finicky if they don't have loose, rich soil in which to enlarge unimpeded. Work the soil well; add organic matter (avoid fresh manure, however) or sand to lighten clay soil. Grow root crops in wide rows, but thin carefully to avoid overcrowding. Keep these vegetables well supplied with water. Radishes are the first to mature (usually in less than a month), but like virtually all root crops, can be harvested at just about any size. There's nothing more delicious than a plateful of tender fingerling carrots, or a side dish of baby beets.

Vine Crops ‡

Cucumbers
Cantaloupes
Gourds
Pumpkins
Squash
Watermelons

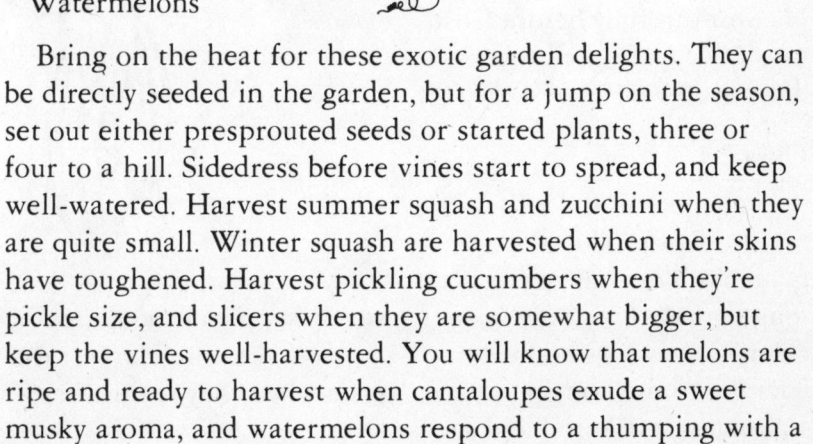

Bring on the heat for these exotic garden delights. They can be directly seeded in the garden, but for a jump on the season, set out either presprouted seeds or started plants, three or four to a hill. Sidedress before vines start to spread, and keep well-watered. Harvest summer squash and zucchini when they are quite small. Winter squash are harvested when their skins have toughened. Harvest pickling cucumbers when they're pickle size, and slicers when they are somewhat bigger, but keep the vines well-harvested. You will know that melons are ripe and ready to harvest when cantaloupes exude a sweet musky aroma, and watermelons respond to a thumping with a

Bountiful Vegetable Gardens

hollow report. In both cases, the attached stems will be thoroughly dried. Gourds and pumpkins can remain in the garden until their vines have died back.

Sweet Corn ‡

You'll need quite a bit of room in your garden for a decent stand of corn. Plant in blocks of several rows for good pollination. Sidedress when silk appears, keep well-watered, and harvest when ears have filled out and silk has turned brown.

Sweet Potatoes ‡

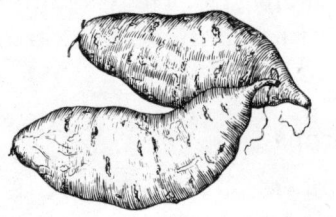

A southern delight, sweet potatoes are grown from "slips"—young plants sprouted from mature sweet potatoes. Slips can be purchased or grown at home. Plant slips in ridges, and fertilize lightly. Make sure the soil is loose to allow for proper root development. Harvest carefully before frost on a dry day; bruised tubers don't keep well.

Okra ‡

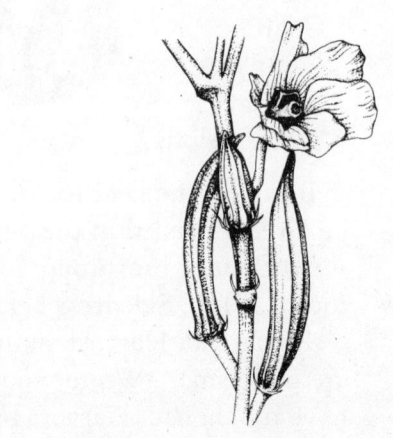

A member of the Hibiscus family, okra produces gorgeous blossoms over a long period. If for only its color, okra is a welcome addition to the home garden. It requires fertile soil and a steady supply of moisture for good production. Harvest the pods when they're 2 inches long.

The Garden Plan

Start small. The amount of available land usually determines how large your garden will be. But even if you have acres to spare, keep in mind that there's nothing more frustrating than not being able to keep up with what you've planted. The well-tended small garden will prove to be more productive in the long run than the large unattended one. A plot 25 by 30 feet is just about the right size to feed a family of four.

25' x 30' Garden With Succession Planting

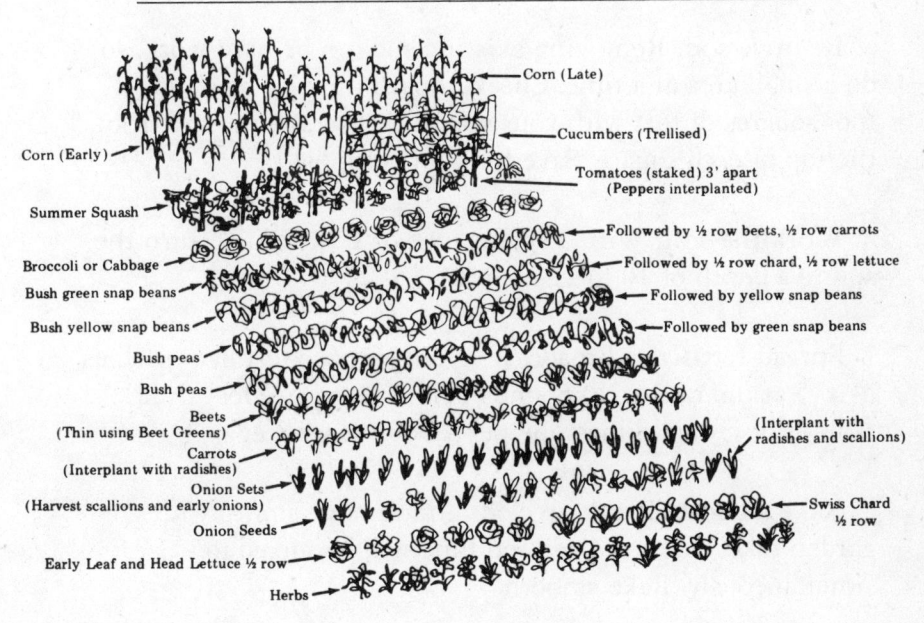

- Corn (Early)
- Summer Squash
- Broccoli or Cabbage
- Bush green snap beans
- Bush yellow snap beans
- Bush peas
- Bush peas
- Beets (Thin using Beet Greens)
- Carrots (Interplant with radishes)
- Onion Sets (Harvest scallions and early onions)
- Onion Seeds
- Early Leaf and Head Lettuce ½ row
- Herbs

- Corn (Late)
- Cucumbers (Trellised)
- Tomatoes (staked) 3' apart (Peppers interplanted)
- Followed by ½ row beets, ½ row carrots
- Followed by ½ row chard, ½ row lettuce
- Followed by yellow snap beans
- Followed by green snap beans
- (Interplant with radishes and scallions)
- Swiss Chard ½ row

• • •

Put it on paper. Whatever the size of your garden, start by sketching where you would like each herb and vegetable to go. How much to plant of each is often a matter of choice, but the chart below will provide you with a rough guide. Make a

Bountiful Vegetable Gardens 51

second sketch that shows what crops will follow when certain vegetables have stopped producing. For example, when your peas are harvested and the vines are turned over, follow with a late planting of carrots.

Planting Techniques

Get started out in the garden as soon as the ground has dried out enough to be worked. If you leave shiny footprints in the soil, it's still too wet. But if a handful of squeezed soil breaks apart with the touch of your thumb, the time is right!

• • •

Stake out your plot. With four pegs and a ball of twine, stake out your garden plot.

• • •

Remove sod. Removing existing sod can be hard work, so do a small area at a time. Checkerboard the plot by slicing 1-foot squares of turf with your spade, and scrape the sod from the top of each square. Save for your compost.

• • •

Work the soil. With a spade, fork or power tiller, turn the soil to a depth of 10 to 12 inches.

• • •

Spread fertilizer. Broadcast an all-purpose fertilizer such as 5-10-5 at the rate of 40 pounds per 1,000 square feet. Add 25 pounds of ground limestone per 1,000 square feet.

• • •

Rake smooth. Break up clods and remove stones with garden rake. The fertilizer and lime will be mixed in simultaneously. Rake smooth.

Use a garden rake to prepare the garden for planting, and also to cover wide rows of seeds with soil.

Stake and make rows. Drive a short stake at the end of each row and stretch a string between them. Make a seed furrow with the corner of your hoe.

Drop seeds. Drop or place seeds into an open furrow, spacing correctly for the variety you are sowing.

Cover with soil. Rake soil over the seed and tap firmly with hoe or rake.

Make transplant holes. With a hand trowel dig out properly spaced holes for all of your transplants (tomatoes, peppers, cabbages, broccoli, etc.). Remove plants from their containers, and set them a little deeper in the ground than they were in their pots. Fill in holes and press soil firmly around stems to eliminate air pockets.

Water, Water. Give the ground a good soaking, making sure the soil doesn't dry out before seeds have germinated.

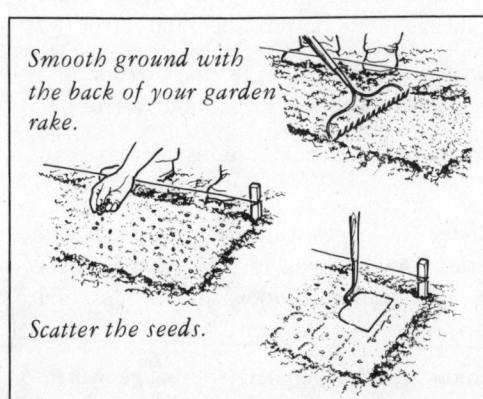

Smooth ground with the back of your garden rake.

Scatter the seeds.

Tap the seeds firmly into the soil with a hoe or rake.

Wide Rows

Instead of planting only single file rows, try some wide rows with just about any crop. Wide rows make efficient use of valuable garden space, save time planting (you can broadcast the seed), and cut down on weeding time since the dense growth crowds out weeds.

Vegetable Helpers

Plant the easy-to-grow herbs below near the appropriate vegetables and fruits to protect them organically from disease and insects. This is called **companion planting** — it helps plants stay strong, and provides you with quantities of healthy vegetables, fruits, and herbs.

Herb	Companions
Basil	Companion to tomatoes, *dislikes* rue. Repels flies and mosquitoes.
Catnip	Plant in border; deters flea beatle.
Chives	Companion to carrots.
Dill	Companion to cabbage; *dislikes* carrots.
Garlic	Plant near roses and raspberries; deters Japanese beetle.
Marigolds	Plant throughout garden; it discourages Mexican bean beetles, nematodes, and other insects. The workhorse of companion plants.
Mint	Companion to cabbage and tomatoes; deters white cabbage moth.
Nasturtium	Companion to radishes, cabbage, and cucumbers; plant under fruit trees. Deters aphids, squash bugs, striped pumpkin beetles.
Petunia	Companion to beans.
Rosemary	Companion to cabbage, beans, carrots, and sage; deters cabbage moth, bean beetles, and carrot fly.
Sage	Plant with rosemary, cabbage, and carrots; *dislikes* cucumbers. Deters cabbage moth, carrot fly.
Summer Savory	Companion to beans and onions; deters bean beetles.
Tansy	Plant under fruit trees; companion to roses and raspberries. Deters flying insects, Japanese beetles, striped cucumber beetles, squash bugs, and ants.
Thyme	Companion to cabbage; deters cabbage worm.
Yarrow	Plant along borders, paths, and near aromatic herbs; enhances production of essential oils.

How to Start Seeds Indoors

A favorite practice of gardeners everywhere is that of starting plants from seeds indoors for transplant in the garden when the air and soil have warmed up. Also called transplants, you can get a head start on the gardening season by starting your flowers and vegetables anywhere from four months to three weeks before you set them in the ground.

The reasons for starting your own plants are many:

- Plants will, in general, be larger, healthier, and hardier.
- You have more control over the size of the plants when you set them out.
- You will be able to choose your favorite varieties from the wide selection available at garden centers and through seed catalogs.
- You can protect plants from diseases and other harmful elements.
- Cost: you can buy a packet of 100 seeds for as much as it would cost you to buy a flat of six plants at the garden center.

There are some flower and vegetable varieties, however, that do not like to be transplanted. Read the seed packet for planting specifics. Root crops and nasturtiums are two examples of plants that will do best if you seed them directly into the space they will occupy in your garden.

The plants you start inside will give you the pleasure of working with a little bit of spring in the midst of winter. Just follow the directions below, and you can look forward to bountiful harvests and spectacular flowers, while at the same time you enjoy indoor gardening until spring and summer beckon.

Pick the Right Medium

Probably the most important aspect of starting seeds inside is the soil mix you choose. Prepared soil mix is probably your best bet for young seedlings because it is sterile (which prevents disease), does not contain weed seeds that can crowd out young plants, holds moisture well, and has enough fertilizer for plants to get off to a good start. Buy a brand that is organic, contains peat and other nutrients, and is pH corrected.

Planting Seeds

You can start seeds in shallow flats or pots, but before you lay in the soil be sure that the flat has been thoroughly cleaned and dried—this will kill any disease organisms. Lay in enough soil so that it is only slightly lower than the top edge of the container. Before you plant any seeds give the soil a good drink and give it enough time to soak in. Some prepared soil mixes are dry at first. Sow seeds in shallow furrows 1 inch apart or according to the instructions on the seed packet. It might be helpful to lay a small piece of chicken wire onto the soil as a guide. This will give you approximately 1-inch squares. Lay a seed or two into each square. Give plants plenty of room—if they have been crowded at this early stage they may not develop properly for successful transplanting.

Again, refer to the seed packet for instructions on whether the seeds can be covered with soil when they are first started. Most seeds need to be covered with a thin layer of soil. But others have to be exposed directly to the light for germination, and are just pressed lightly into the soil and not covered. Once you have sown the seeds water them lightly, but do not soak them. Cover the flat with plastic wrap to hold in the moisture at this crucial stage. Do not completely seal the plastic to the flat. A little air is needed for circulation, and to prevent damping-off disease. Remove the film only when the first seedlings appear.

Label everything clearly with the name of the plant and the date the seeds went in.

Temperature and Lighting

Young plants need warmth and plenty of light. Just after seeds have been started it is best that the temperature be kept relatively constant, so it might be a good idea to have a room thermometer to monitor any change in temperature. From the time that they are planted until their first set of true leaves develops, seedlings prefer a temperature between 75 and 80°F. After plants have developed, they will grow best in cooler temperatures: about 70° during the day, and 60° at night.

Choose a good sunny spot for your flats so they may enjoy as much natural sunlight as possible, but move the plants away from cold windows at night to a warm place. Keep plants out of cool, drafty places as much as possible.

Constant artificial light at the early stages of growth would be ideal. Set up some lamps near or just above the surface on which your plants are growing. It has been found that artificial light for 14 to 16 hours a day will help produce strong, compact plants. After about four weeks, natural light will suffice.

Watering and Fertilizing

The amount and manner of watering seedlings are much in dispute, but it seems that the most successful methods are simple: use water that is just on the verge of being warm (do not use cold water), and give your seedlings frequent light waterings every day with a mister or bulb-type sprinkler. The trick is to give the plants enough water so that they make strong early growth, but not so much that they become waterlogged.

Fertilize your plants once a week after the seedlings have been up a week or two.

Transplanting

Once your plants have grown inside for the proper amount of time you must prepare them for their life outdoors. This process is known as hardening off, and it takes a week or two depending on the natural hardiness of the plant.

While they are still in flats, place plants in a cold frame outside. Keep the lid closed at first, then gradually expose the plants to wind and sun for a longer time each day. If you don't have a cold frame, move the plants from the house to a shady, protected area during the day and bring them inside at night. Move them out into full sunlight over a period of time, and then leave them overnight when you feel they are ready.

After each set of flats has been carefully hardened off (meaning there is no evidence that the plants have been weakened), and if there is no threat of frost, you can plant them in your garden. Prepare the soil for your transplants: it should be light, loamy, and well-cultivated to a depth of at least 10 inches.

Insulated cold frame.

When to Sow Vegetable and Flower Seeds Indoors

Vegetable	Weeks before setting out
Onions, leeks	10-12
Celery	8-10
Tomatoes	6-8
Eggplant	6-8
Peppers	4-6
Cabbage	4-6
Cauliflower	4-6
Broccoli	4-6
Head lettuce	3-4
Melons & cucumbers*	3-4

*Must be started in individual containers and transplanted without disturbing roots.

Flower	Weeks before setting out
Begonias	12-15
Gloxinias	12-15
Giant Dahlias	10-12
Impatiens	10-12
Pansies	10-12
Seed Geraniums	10-12
Petunias	10-12
Tall Marigolds	10-12
Asters	6-8
Bachelor's Buttons	6-8
Coleus	6-8
Portulaca	6-8
Snapdragons	6-8
Zinnias	6-8
Alyssum	3-4
Dwarf Marigolds	3-4
Other annuals	3-4

Caring for Growing Plants

Thin, thin, thin! Thin emerging seedlings according to spacing directions. Be heartless; the survivors will thank you for it later.

• • •

Keep the water coming. Most crops require about 1 inch of water weekly. Keep a few pans around and see how much collects after a rain or a sprinkling.

• • •

Feed plants when they blossom. As plants begin to blossom and set fruit, or as leaf crops approach maturity, they need a boost. Sidedress them with a few pinches of fertilizer.

• • •

Weed, weed, weed! Weeds rob plants of water and nutrients. Cultivate regularly to remove growing weeds and to kill weed seedlings that are always ready to emerge—especially after a rain.

–7–

SIMPLE WEED AND PEST CONTROL

Prevention is *always* the first line of defense against problems in the garden. Incorporate these seven steps into your gardening program for worry-free seasons of bountiful harvests.

Healthy Soil, Healthy Plants

Garden soil enriched by large amounts of organic matter will produce healthy, robust plants. And it is well-known that insects rarely attack strong plants, choosing instead to prey on weak, spindly ones—a form of natural selection. A vigilant soil-building program, therefore, such as the one outlined in chapter 2, is the first and best defense against serious insect and disease infestation.

Rotate Your Crops Out of Harm's Way

Changing the location of your crops from year to year can be an extremely effective measure against heavy insect and disease invasion. Many insects depend on a single host plant for their food supply. For example, moving your cabbages this year to the other side of the garden might well deny the newly hatched cabbage worms the food necessary for their growth.

Nobody has a perfect memory—it's impossible to remember which vegetable or flower grew where from one year to the next. So make an accurate chart, and keep it in a safe place for handy annual reference.

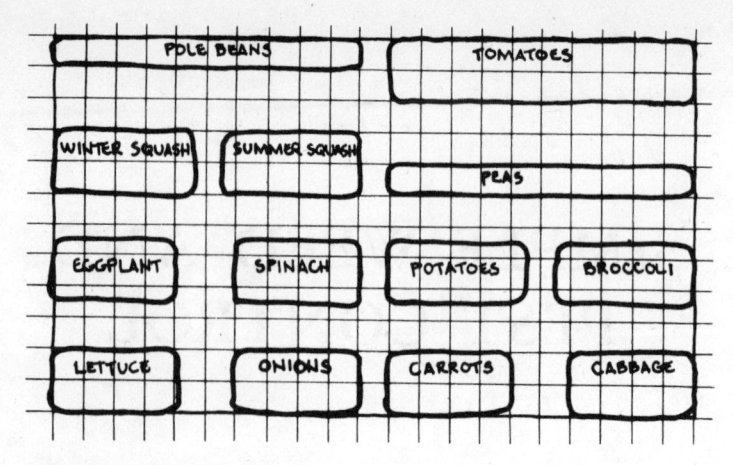

A sample garden chart. Make one every year, and don't lose it!

Garden Hygiene: Clean Up Your Act

Nothing encourages the successful wintering-over of certain insect populations and disease organisms like standing crop residues. So when your corn is picked, pull up the stalks while they are still green, chop them up, and either till them under or throw them on the compost pile. A rototiller will usually make short work of pea and bean vines, and even the root stalks of harvested cabbage, broccoli, cauliflower, and brussels sprouts. But if you don't have a tiller, uproot anything left after harvest and toss it in the compost.

It is a wise practice to cut down tall grass and weeds that surround your garden. This high growth is a haven for many insects and small animals.

Create A Balanced Environment In Your Garden

If you're giving away a good thing, a lot of people are going to show up at your doorstep. Likewise, when farmers grow huge fields of cotton, it's no wonder that cotton weevils turn out in force. Take a lesson here for your garden. Not that your garden will allow for endless rows of a single crop, but no law says that, even on a small scale, you have to plant all your corn in one location. Diversify your plants and their locations. If, for example, your garden plan calls for two rows of beans, try planting two different varieties in separate sections.

Use Pest and Disease Resistant Varieties

In recent years, plant breeders have developed many varieties of popular garden crops that are resistant to many common insects and diseases. Planting resistant varieties, therefore, is probably the simplest way to prevent heavy infestations. Refer to the list below of vegetable varieties that have been specially bred to resist disease and punishment by the weather. In parenthesis is the company from which you can obtain the seeds.

Asparagus

1 Viking: The hardy, improved, rust-tolerant strain used by commercial growers (Stokes).
1 B Viking KB3: Much hardier in sub zero or hot desert climates—and shows greater rust and fusarium tolerance than all-male clones of F1 hybrids. Now considered the best O.P. by growers in China, Taiwan, Japan, California, Mexico, Michigan, and Canada (Stokes).
Mary Washington: Older variety, still popular, highly resistant to rust (Burpee, Parks).

Bean

Greensleeves: Resistant to common and New York 15 bean mosaic (Burpee exclusive).
Tendercrop: Disease resistant (Park's).
Triumph: Resistant to common bean mosaic (Farmers).
Harvester: Disease resistant (Twilley, Stokes).

Bean, dry shell

Great Northern: Disease resistant (Farmers).
Bush Fava Bean, Long Pod, or English Broadbean: Much hardier than other beans; successful substitute for lima beans in the north (Burpee).

Cabbage

Stokes Viking Golden Acre: High yellows tolerance (Stokes).
Regalia, early hybrid: Yellows tolerant and good tolerance to bursting in the field (Stokes).
Heavyweighter Hybrid: Very resistant to both heat and frost (Park's).
Early Jersey Wakefield, Golden Acre, Tastie Hybrid and Stonehead Hybrid: Yellows resistant (Burpee).

Cucumber

Early Pride Hybrid, Streamliner Hybrid: Tolerant to mildew and mosaic. *"Burpless" Hybrids, Sweet Slice Hybrid:* Tolerant to downy and powdery mildew, leaf spot, mosaic, anthracnose and scab. *Sweet Success Hybrid:* Resistant to cucumber and watermelon viruses, scab and leaf spot, tolerant to powdery and downy mildews. (All from Burpee)
Bush Whopper: Disease resistant. *Sweet Success Hybrid:* Resistant to cucumber mosaic virus, scab and target leaf spot. (Both from Park's)
Ultraslice tm Early: Good under stress weather conditions, and the ultimate in disease tolerance (Stokes).

Eggplant

Dusky: Good TVM tolerance, green calyx. *French Imperial:* TVM tolerance. (Both from Stokes)

Kale

Dwarf Blue Curled Vates: Withstands heavy frosts (Park's).
Green Curled Scotch: Harvest after frost (Stokes).

Lettuce

Oakleaf: Hot weather resistant. *Buttercrunch:* Remains sweet even after plant goes to seed. *Summer Boston:* Slow bolting. (All from Stokes)
Butter King, Bibb, or *Limestone:* Hot weather tolerant (Shumway).

Green Ice: Slow to go to seed (Burpee exclusive).
Red Sails: Slow to go to seed. *Minetto:* Resistant to tip burn. (Both from Burpee)

Muskmelon

Luscious Hybrid: Resistant to wilt and highly tolerant of powdery mildew. *Short 'n' Sweet:* Heat, drought, and disease resistant. (Both from Burpee)
Mainerock: Strong fusarium resistance (Farmer's).
Supermarket Hybrid: Strong resistance to fusarium and mildew (Farmer's).
Burpee's Ambrosia Hybrid: Resistant to powdery mildew (Burpee exclusive).

Peas

Wando: Tolerant to heat and cold. *Freezonian:* Wilt-resistant. *Green Arrow:* Resistant to downy mildew and fusarium wilt. (All from Burpee)
Sugar Daddy: The first stringless pea. *Sugar Snap:* Frost tolerant. *Sugarann:* Resistant to powdery mildew. (All from Park's)
Fridget: Resistant to fusarium wilt, race 1 (Harris).
Green Arrow: Disease resistant. *Dark-Skin Perfection:* Heat resistant. *Snowflake:* Resistant to wilt and powdery mildew. (All from Field's)

Pepper

Keystone Giant: Foliage abundant, protects from sunburn (Field's).
Ma Belle: TVM resistant. *Bell Boy:* Drought resistant and does well in dry weather. *Blocker:* TVM resistant. (All from Twilley)
Park's Whopper Hybrid: Weather resistant (Park exclusive).
Golden Summer Hybrid: New lush foliage protects from sunscald, Tobacco Mosaic resistant (Park's).
Valley Giant Hybrid: TVM resistant. *Big Bertha:* TVM resistant. (Both from Twilley)

Weed and Pest Control

Radish

Cherry Beauty: 1st hybrid red radish, slow to turn pithy (Twilley).
Scarlet Knight: Fusarium tolerant, good type for warm weather (Twilley).
Champion: Thrives in cool weather. *Red Baron:* Seldom cracks, good disease resistance. (Both from Field's)
Easter Egg: Grows large without becoming pithy (Burpee).

Spinach

America: Slow to bolt. *Winter Bloomsdale:* Blight resistant, slow to bolt. *Melody Hybrid:* Resistant to downy mildew, mosaic. (All from Burpee)
Bloomsdale Long-Standing: Early maturity, slow to bolt (Field's).
Hybrid USDA No. 7: Early maturing, very vigorous (Farmer's).
Melody Hybrid: Disease resistant, early maturity (Park's).

Sweet Corn

Florida Staysweet: Highly disease resistant. *Butterfruit:* Super-sweet, strong germination (Park's exclusive).
Kandy Korn EH: Stays sweeter longer (Field's).
Burpee's Honeycross: Extra seedling vigor, wilt-resistant (Burpee).
Silver Queen: Disease tolerant (Burpee, Park's).
Northern Sweet Hybrid: Retains sweetness for long period (Farmer's).
Summer Sweet: Multi-ear under good fertility (Twilley).

Tomatoes

Liberty: Disease resistant. *Big Seven Hybrid, Indeterminate:* Resistant to three diseases. (Both from Twilley)
Supersonic: Fusarium resistant race 1, and verticillium wilt (Harris).

Jet Star: Fusarium resistant, race 1, and verticillium wilt (Harris).
Floramerica: Tolerates 17 plant diseases (Farmer's).
Delicious: This is the seed which produced the world's largest tomato, 6 lbs. 8 oz., and listed in the *Guinness Book of World Records* (Burpee).

Turnip

Tokyo Cross: Good resistance to virus and other diseases (Burpee).

Watermelon

Super Sweet Seedless Hybrid: Seedless and crisp, needs standard variety for pollination (Park's).
Petite Sweet: Disease resistant. *Sweetmeat:* Highly tolerant to fusarium. (Both from Farmer's)
Charleston Gray: Fusarium resistant, anthracnose, and sunburn resistant (Burpee).
Crimson Sweet: Fusarium wilt, and anthracnose resistant (Burpee).
Jubilee: Rattlesnake type; fusarium and anthracnose resistant (Field's).

Of course this does not by any means exhaust the list of disease resistant varieties. Many other seed companies carry these varieties as well, unless noted as an exclusive. All varieties taken from catalogs of the various companies.

Outsmart the Bugs

Planting crops earlier or later than usual—whenever possible—will discourage the normal breeding cycle of some insects and allow your plants to make it safely beyond the vulnerable seedling stage without major insect attack. Get your greens and cole crops going as soon as the ground can be worked, and they'll be in good shape by the time the predators hatch out and begin their hungry search for food.

Create Barriers

Cutworms and wireworms are notorious for their love of young seedlings and transplants. During the night, they encircle the tender stems and scissor them off at ground level. Next morning, the dismayed gardener sees a row of fallen plants.

Cutworm "collars" are pieces of paper or thin cardboard that are wrapped around the bottom 2 inches of the plant stem before it is set in the ground, and they make it impossible for these stealthy worms to do their nocturnal destruction. Placing a toothpick or two around each stem, a twig, an ice cream stick, or even a piece of tar paper will accomplish the same results.

The Facts About Insects

Of every ten living things on earth that you can see with the naked eye, eight of them are insects. In the United States alone, more than 85,000 separate species have been identified. Most of them, according to fossil records, evolved to perfection long before humans began walking erect.

We need insects; without them plant pollination would be spotty or downright impossible. As gardeners, what we don't need, however, are insect attacks that cost us the fruits of our labors.

When bugs show up in your garden, *don't panic*. There are many safe and easy ways to control their numbers and destruction.

Strategies for Insect Control

Handpicking. Removing insects by hand from your garden will reduce their numbers in short order. Many insects, particularly during their larval or "worm" stages, are slow-moving and can be picked off their host plants quite easily. Gardeners should do a great deal of inspecting anyway, especially early in the season. As you walk along your rows of plants and flower beds, carry a coffee can one-third full of kerosene or paint thinner. When you spot a bug (leave the ladybugs alone, they're friends), pick it off and drop it into the can. Wear gloves for the job; you never know when you'll run into blister beetles.

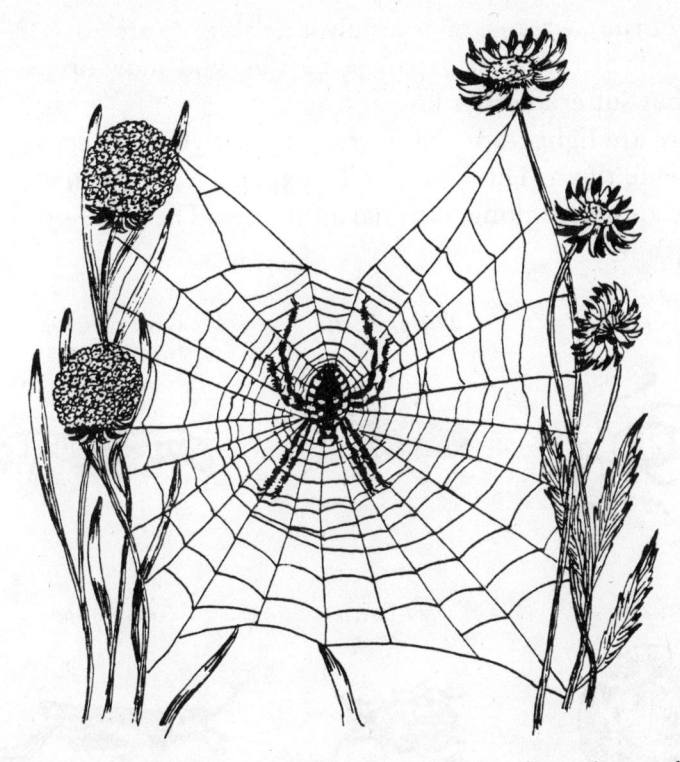

After dark is the best time to hunt for cutworms. Scratch the surface around plant stems; exposed to the beam of your flashlight, cutworms will curl up. Drop them into the kerosene. Some varieties of cutworm feed higher up on plants, so check there too.

• • •

Trapping insects. Another way to render insects harmless is to lure them into traps. A little beer in a dish or small pie tin will entice slugs in and kill them. Thin wads of yeasty dough strewn about will achieve the same results.

Wooden boards strewn with large cabbage and lettuce leaves will attract slugs and other pests. Lift the boards in the heat of the day and see who's come to get out of the sun. Drop the trouble-makers into your kerosene can.

Weed and Pest Control

Sex hormone traps, now widely available, create an irresistible attraction to Japanese beetles who show up to mate, but suffer another fate entirely.

There are light traps that attract night-flying insects and electrocute them. These tend to be expensive, and will zap beneficial insects along with harmful ones. The trade-off may be worth it.

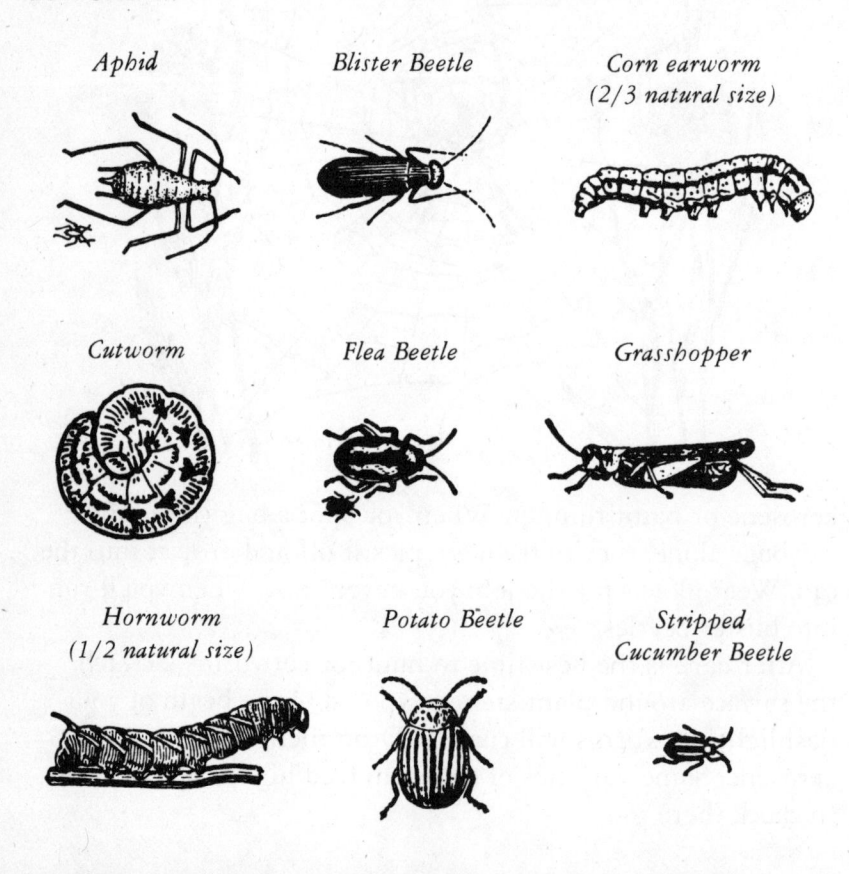

Aphid

Blister Beetle

Corn earworm
(2/3 natural size)

Cutworm

Flea Beetle

Grasshopper

Hornworm
(1/2 natural size)

Potato Beetle

Stripped Cucumber Beetle

Controlling insects biologically. Many insects in the garden do a great deal to keep down the pest population. It's well-known that ladybugs thrive on aphids, alfalfa weevils, Colorado potato beetles, and other soft-bodied insects. You can actually *buy* ladybugs from companies that advertise in gardening magazines. A pint container holds 8,000 ladybugs, and each ladybug will devour fifty aphids daily. One pint is sufficient for a 40 by 50 foot garden.

Other beneficial insects available for purchase are *lacewing flies*, which can consume hundreds of plant lice in a day; the *praying mantis*, which devours caterpillars, mites, and other large insects; and *trichogamma wasps*, parasites which lay their eggs on the eggs or larvae of harmful insects. Each can be ordered by mail and will arrive with instructions for introducing them into your garden. Check with your Cooperative Extension Service for details.

Another method of biological insect control is *bacillus thuringiensis*, a disease organism that will attack and destroy harmful insects when sprayed or dusted on affected plants. It is commonly sold as Dipel or Thurecide.

Beneficial Insects

Insect	Benefit
Braconid Wasps	Females lay eggs in body of tomato hornworm which the larvae then consume as their first meals.
Lacewing Fly	Thrives on aphids. Pale green, fly-like bug.
Calosoma Beetle	Hard-shelled, 2 inches long, loves to eat caterpillars.
Hover Fly	Larvae of this four-winged fly feed on aphids and scale insects.
Ichneumon Fly	Lays eggs in caterpillars and their pupae, which the young flies then consume.
Ladybug	Eats its weight in aphids daily.
Praying Mantis	Up to 3 inches long; feasts on pests, including mosquitoes.
Spiders	Many arachnids subsist on garden pests.
Wheel Bug	Gray, 1½ inches long, preys on soft-shelled pests; in profile it looks as if a cogged wheel were attached to its back.

• • •

Home brews and sprays. For centuries gardeners have experimented with home-brewed insect repellants. Even today, there are gardeners who swear by their concoctions. Since half the fun of gardening lies in experimenting, you might want to brew up a batch of your own.

As for recipes, one guiding principle is that insects tend to dislike pungent smells, which leaves the way open for any number of onion/garlic/hot pepper/soap combinations. Whatever the ingredients, run them through the blender with a little water, strain carefully, pour the liquid into a sprayer, and apply to infested plants. Reapply regularly, especially after a rain.

Another old standby is lime water. In a large mixing container pour a gallon of water over a shovelful of garden lime or wood ashes. Let the mixture stand until the lime or ashes have settled to the bottom. Pour off clear liquid into a hand or pump sprayer and apply to areas of infestation.

Finally (though this list is by no means complete), a relatively recent "bug juice" theory holds that the *decomposed bodies of insects blended with water*, strained thoroughly to avoid clogging the sprayer, and doused over affected plants, will send harmful insects scurrying.

Let your imagination be your guide in this area. Who knows? You might come up with the ultimate insect repellant!

• • •

Chemical control of insects. Commercially prepared insecticides are effective weapons against serious insect attacks, and are safe when handled and applied according to directions. There are three distinct types: 1.) *the botanicals*, manufactured from naturally occurring substances such as rotenone, pyrethrum, and nicotene; 2.) *the inorganics*, or metal derivatives; and 3.) *the synthetic organics*, which are the most popular.

If you are going to do *any* spraying or dusting, it is essential that you have proper equipment for the job. Anything makeshift can be hazardous to your health. The illustrated chart offers many possibilities.

Rules for Safe Handling, Use, and Storage of Chemicals and Spraying Equipment

1. Be sure that all chemicals, whether they are insecticides, fungicides, or herbicides, are clearly labelled POISONOUS, and kept well out of the reach of children, pets, and livestock. Store them safely away from food or animal feed.
2. Always read the directions label, and follow safety and application procedures to the letter.
3. Don't smoke when spraying or dusting.
4. Always wear a mask when spraying or dusting, and otherwise avoid inhaling chemical fumes and dusts.
5. Avoid spills. If skin contact is made, wash the exposed areas thoroughly, according to directions on the chemical container.
6. Discard empty containers in thick plastic garbage bags and bring to the local dump or compacter.
7. Never put pesticides or other chemicals in glass containers.
8. To avoid residue problems on edible crops, be sure you spray or dust only in the recommended period prior to harvest.
9. Store spraying and dusting equipment in a safe place that is inaccessible to children. Wash all equipment thoroughly at the end of the growing season.

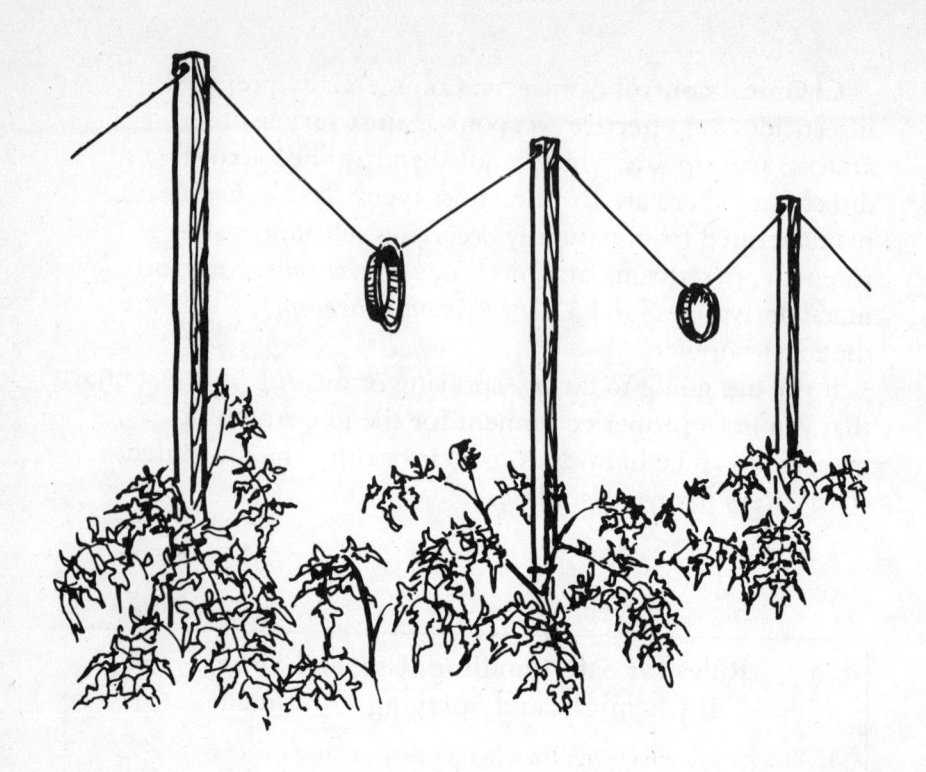

Pie plates foil the birds.

—8—

EASY MAINTENANCE OF TREES AND SHRUBS

The dictionary defines "maintain" as *providing against failure and decline*. And when it comes to trees and shrubbery, truer words were never spoken.

There are many ways to approach maintenance, but there is no reason to see the chores as anything but quite simple. Some of the work is done during the active growing season as part of normal care, but other maintenance tasks are performed in the "off-season."

Pruning

Pruning of trees and shrubs is performed for five reasons:

1. It promotes flowering and fruiting.
2. Pruning balances root mass to top growth when transplanting.
3. Pruning removes dead or injured branches and reduces disease susceptibility.
4. Pruning controls the growth and shape of trees and shrubs.
5. Pruning can renew old plantings.

Tools You'll Need

Pruning shears. This is the most used, and useful, tool for fine pruning of shrubs, and for rough work such as cutting roots.

Long-handled lopping shears. These will give you additional leverage and reach for taller or bigger branches.

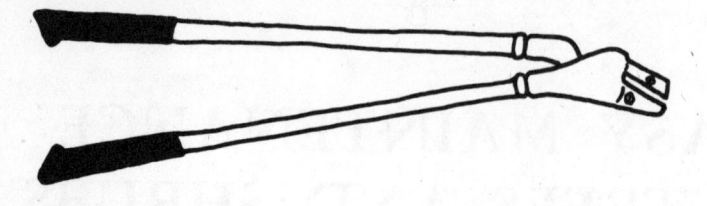

A tree pruner. A set of pruning shears mounted on a pole for cutting very high branches. Cutting is activated by a rope and spring.

A pruning saw. Either straight-bladed or curved for general work, or fine-toothed for finer work. A **bow saw** is handy for bucking up large branches. A **pole saw** is similar to a pole pruner—it is a saw mounted on a long pole.

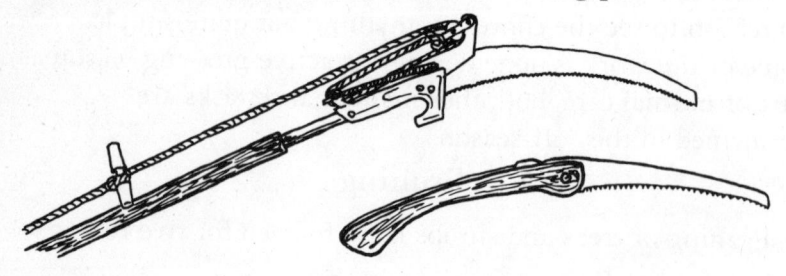

A sharp knife. Another essential for trimming tree wounds left when branches have been removed.

A long-handled hedge-shear. Electric or hand-powered, it is used for cutting the softer growth of hedges.

Keep all tools clean and sharp. Lubricate clippers and

pruners. Protect metal surfaces from rust by keeping them dry and oiled. Clean off sap and pitch from pruning tools with kerosene or alcohol. And wear a good pair of gloves to prevent blisters and keep tools from slipping out of wet hands.

When Should You Prune?

There are no hard and fast rules that cover every kind of tree and plant growth. Trees are usually pruned when they are dormant. If pruned in spring, or even late winter, certain trees will bleed too much sap. Others, if pruned in the summer or early fall, may develop new soft growth that won't withstand the winter. For these reasons, vines (such as grapevines) are also pruned when they are dormant. But hedges, on the other hand, are trimmed several times each growing season to stimulate denser growth.

With flowering shrubs, you need to know whether blooms will form on year-old growth or on new growth. Prune in early spring to stimulate growth for shrubs that will bloom on new shoots; but pruning *after* flowering is best for shrubs such as forsythia that bloom on year-old wood. In any case, check with a local nurseryman if you have questions about when and how much to prune your shrubs.

How To Prune

The cardinal rule of pruning is *cut cleanly and leave no stubs*. A dead stub is vulnerable to infection that can spread to the rest of the tree. The second cardinal rule is *either cut close to the main branch or immediately above a bud*.

Only one of these stubs has been pruned properly. Left to right: the first cut is correct; the second leaves too much surface exposed; the third cut leaves a stub that is too long from the bud; and the fourth cut was made too close to the bud.

Maintenance of Trees and Shrubs

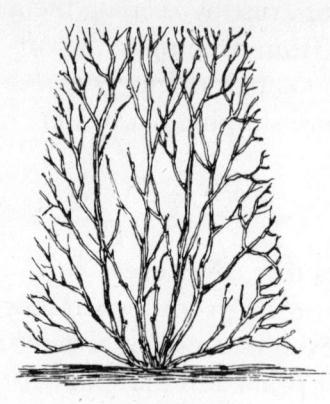

A hedge bush should always be wider at the base than at the top. The hedge bush on the left has been correctly pruned.

Practical Pruning Tips

- Cut off diseased, dead or broken branches from any tree as soon as you notice them.
- Prune the weaker of two rubbing or interfering branches that are developing bark wounds—the quicker the better.
- Always prune flush to the parent branch or trunk. If only the end of a branch is dead, cut just beyond and close to a bud.
- In pruning, don't leave stubs or ragged cuts. Always use sharp, clean-cutting pruning tools.
- All bark wounds over 1 1/2 inches in diameter should have a coating of tree paint or sealer.
- Prune a hedge so that the plants will grow wider at the base than at the top.
- Pruning top terminal branches will produce a low, spreading tree. Pruning lateral or side branches will make the tree grow vertically and more symmetrically.
- Burn all prunings to avoid spreading disease and attracting rot organisms.
- Keep trees out of foundation plantings. Never let trees and shrubs block house windows.
- Keep your feet on the ground. Don't use step ladders or other makeshift stools to reach taller branches. Use long-handled tree pruners and pole saws. If you cannot reach the very top of the trees, call in someone with the proper equipment.

Pruning A Young Fruit Tree

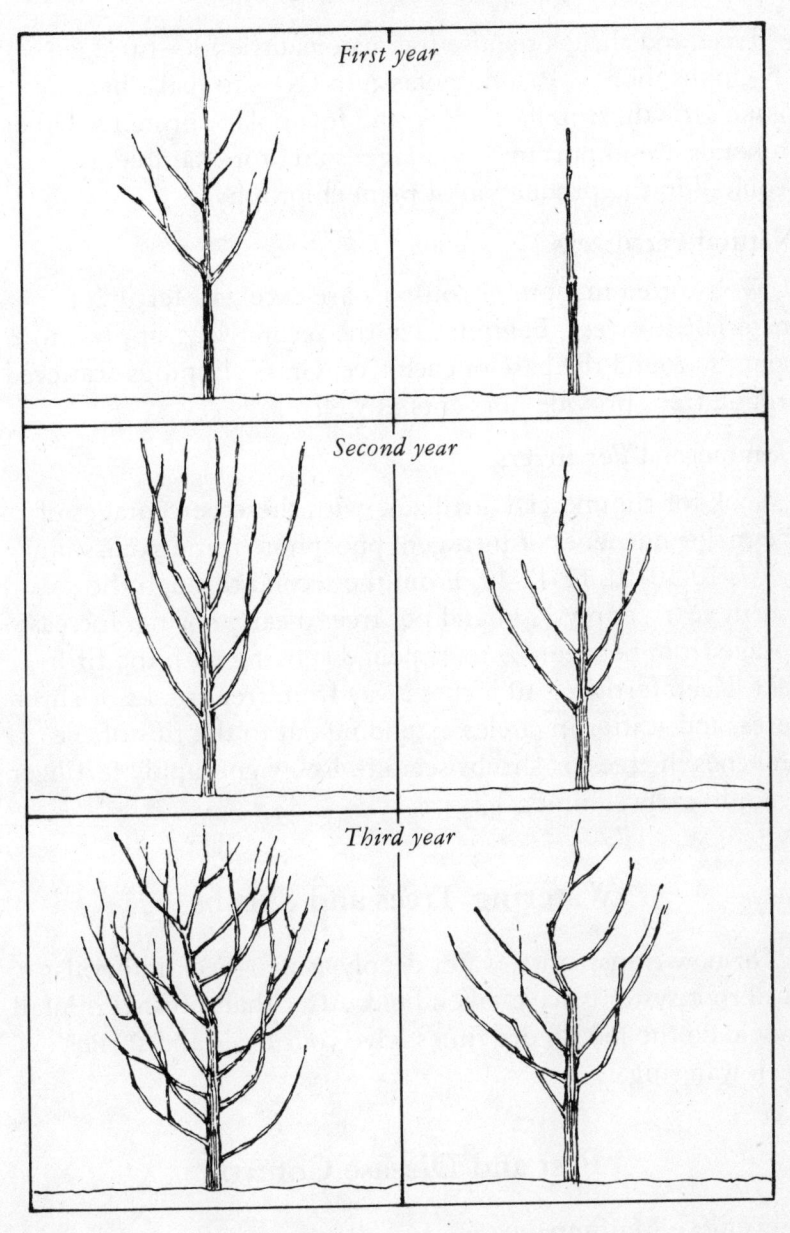

First year

Second year

Third year

You have to prune a young fruit tree to develop a strong central leader. In its first year, it is cut back to a strong leader; in the second year, primary scaffold branches are allowed to develop; by the third year it has reached its mature form.

Feeding Trees and Shrubs

Trees and shrubs require the major nutrients—nitrogen (N), phosphorus (P), and potassium (K)—to make healthy tissue growth, stimulate roots, and form plant proteins. Other minerals are important too. Magnesium, for example, is required in the production of plant chlorophyll.

Natural Fertilizers

Well-rotted manure or compost are excellent fertilizing materials for trees. Beginning in the second year, apply 1 to 2 pounds around the base of each tree. Grass clippings scattered around trees provide nutrients as well.

Commercial Fertilizers

Look for commercial fertilizers with these percentages of the major nutrients of nitrogen, phosphorus, and potassium: 5-8-7, 10-10-10, 12-12-12. From the second through the fourth years, apply ¼ pound per tree in early spring. Increase dosage from between ½ to ¾ pound starting with the fifth year. Keep fertilizer 10 inches away from tree trunks or shrub bases, and scatter in circles extending out to the tips of the branches. If trees or shrubs seem to lack vigor, apply fertilizer again in early summer.

Watering Trees and Shrubs

For new transplants, water deeply at two-week intervals until root systems have taken hold. After that, normal rainfall should do the job. In dry times, give your trees and shrubs deep watering.

Pest and Disease Control

Preventive Maintenance

The first line of defense against invasions of insects and disease is always care, cleanliness, and a little planning. Here are some clean-up procedures to follow:

- Cut out and burn all dead and diseased wood.
- Remove and destroy all dropped wood and fruit.
- Remove all mummied fruit from trees, vines, and shrubs.
- Scrape loose bark for trunks, crotches, and main limbs—especially on apple trees, to destroy codling moth larvae.
- Use disease resistant varieties.
- Collect and burn debris on the ground in late fall or early spring to destroy hibernating curculios that survive the winter as adults under leaves, grass, bark, and rubbish near trees or in nearby fence rows.

Edging

Edging neatly defines the division between lawn and paths, lawns and borders, borders and walks, and so forth. The division can be marked by the tidy margin of the lawn itself, or by using a variety of edging materials. These include bricks or blocks, narrow wood boards, a concrete curb, or strips of steel or plastic that are widely available at garden centers. You can even use a row of compact low-growing flowering plants to create a well-defined border edge (see page 39, for a list of excellent edging plants).

Spraying

Geography frequently determines the level of insect and disease attack. Your Cooperative Extension office will be of enormous help in planning a control program. See chapter 7 for a list of proper equipment and rules for safe handling of insecticides.

–9–

FINISHING TOUCHES

Okay. The labor is done. The lawn is thick and lush, colorful flowers abound everywhere. The garden is teeming with gorgeous vegetables, and the trees are heavy with fruit. You look around a time or two at your handiwork and think to yourself, what we need now are a few *finishing touches*. What if there were a little fountain over there by the junipers? Or maybe a birdhouse flanking the driveway and perhaps a few feeders thoughtfully placed here and there around the grounds? And, of course, a table and chairs with an umbrella to protect against the strong sun would be perfect when neighbors come to call.

In fact, there is a universe of lovely items to choose from: unique outdoor decorations, clever items of convenience, products to make sitting outdoors and admiring the natural environment you've created ever more comfortable and fun. Here's a partial listing. You might even get an idea or two for things to make on your own.

For the Birds

Bird feeders. They come in a variety of sizes and shapes as you know if you've spent any time at all shopping for them. Some birds prefer dining alone, so you might want to consider multiple feeders. Keep feeders out in the open so the birds can keep their eye on any lurking felines. Here are a few feeders you can make in just a couple of minutes. Keep them well stocked with seed and suet during even the coldest winter, and you'll never lack for lively, chattering companionship.

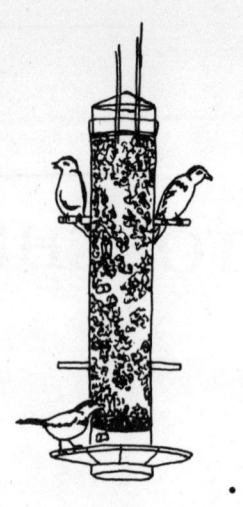

• • •

Birdhouses. Gardeners often disagree about the value of birds congregating around the homestead. Birds will keep down insect populations, but they may help themselves to your berries as a reward for their vigilance. The shrubs and trees you've planted will encourage birds in numbers, but if you want to provide them with special shelter, install a birdhouse. As with all things, you can buy them, or you can build them. In either case, here are some guidelines:

- Keep the colors plain—brilliant colors won't attract birds.
- A birdhouse should face away from the prevailing wind, and be safe from cats.
- If you're installing more than one, keep them separated by a considerable distance to avert bird wars.
- Make sure the house interior is accessible and easy to clean, and that the floor has drainage holes. Also, the house must not tilt upwards or rain may enter and get trapped.

Bird baths. They can be a pleasant addition to any property, but here again, make sure that the bathing beauties are safe from prowling cats.

Sundials. Place one in a spot that gets sun all day; the middle of the vegetable garden is perfect.

Ponds and pools. Water featured in ponds and pools will enhance the loveliness of any property. Pool design should emphasize prominent landscaping features—perhaps an outcropping of stone, or a particularly lovely ornamental tree. Of course, pond and pool construction can involve considerable expense, but there are a number of ways to save money. For example, you don't really need a natural source of water—it can be piped from the house and circulated by a pump, or you can be clever with the garden hose. Check nurseries and specialty supply houses for options.

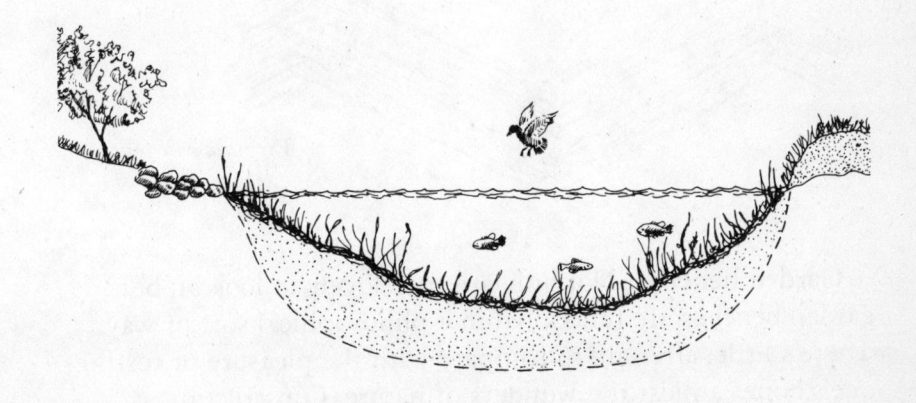

Finishing Touches

Fences. They vary in design depending on the function they're intended to serve. Here are some options to consider:

- board fences
- shingle fences
- basket-weave fences
- stockade fences
- planting fences
- stone fences
- masonry walls
- decorative fences

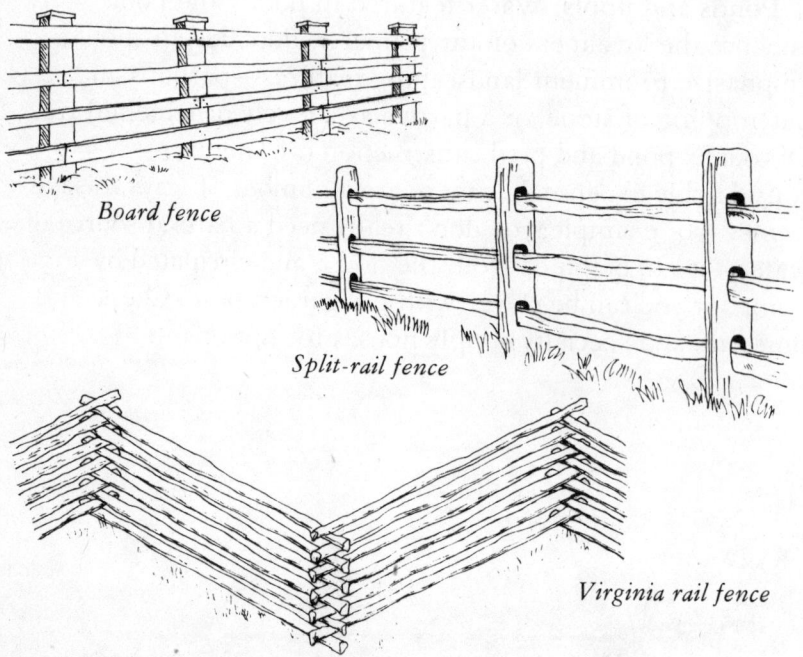

Picket fence

Board fence

Split-rail fence

Virginia rail fence

Garden benches. Not only are they lovely to look at, but garden benches are functional in a philosophical sort of way. There's little, after all, to compare with the pleasure of resting one's bones amidst the wonders of nature. Constructing a solid bench is simple.

Patios and Decks

These are major projects that require substantial planning and investment, but virtually nothing else serves as the perfect finishing touch which will be enjoyed for years to come. Decks are normally of wood construction. A deck can be built to cover a relatively small area—at the back of the house, for instance; or it can be constructed in a series of levels and sprawl as much as your budget will allow. Some of the most beautiful decking incorporates features of the landscape such as fruit and shade trees, and large outcroppings of stone. Even water gardens can be included.

Patios are generally of masonry construction—either cement, bricks, or concrete blocks of one type or another—and can become as much a part of the outdoor environment as natural wood decking.

• • •

Planters, boxes, and hanging baskets. Annual flowers hung in baskets do wonders to beautify the deck and patio areas of any home. Flower boxes placed for effect also lend colorful accents to the outdoor decor. Clever gardeners have learned the value of growing patio vegetables and herbs to save time and trouble when company comes. Need salad fixings? Why, just reach up and pluck off a handful of cherry tomatoes! And why run all the way out to the garden for oregano and basil and dill, when there's a healthy supply of all three growing in planters on the back deck?

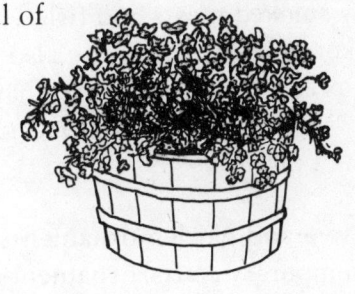

• • •

Shrubs in tubs. Strategically placed near entrances they can be quite striking and lovely. Woodward and pyramidal arborvitae are especially well-suited to tub planting, as are mugho pines which grow to a height of 15 to 18 inches. But if

Finishing Touches

the tub is large enough, and the soil conditions are right, there is no limit to what can be grown—even blueberry bushes!

• • •

Outdoor lighting. Carefully located outdoor lights are indispensable both for safety and beauty. At your electrical supply outlet, you'll find special lights for flower borders, lights which project their beams downward (down lights), and fixtures which project upward (floodlights). For the patio or deck there are wrought iron and paper lanterns, ceramic globes, torches, and many other outdoor lighting fixtures. You might even be able to locate antique gas lamps. Here are some lighting ideas to consider.
- Accent a tree with a white floodlight to show the tree's color.
- Highlight flower borders with a line of ground-level reflecting lights.
- The actual source of light should be a mystery; with a little thought you may find how to hide fixtures from view.
- Light all outdoor steps for safety.

• • •

Outdoor cooking. It can be a seasonal delight when you have the right equipment. Charcoal barbecues are available in dozens of models, from the simple cast iron hibachi to larger more elaborate units capable of roasting a turkey! And if you enjoy smoked meats and fish, you'll find many models of patio smokers as well. There are also gas grills for backyard chefs who prefer not to deal with charcoal, and electric units for cooks who want the heat, but not the flame.

• • •

Lawn and garden ornaments. From fine sculpture to contemporary crafts, ornaments adorn millions of American lawns and gardens. Whether you prefer pink flamingos or oriental statuary—and anything else in between—there is at least one spot on your property that could benefit from this sort of decoration. Even an interestingly shaped piece of driftwood can make a beautiful ornament when put in just the right setting.

Strawberry Boxes, Barrels, and Pyramids

Strawberries are exciting and easy to grow, but not many gardeners have the space for them in the garden. Here's how to grow the most luscious, red-ripe berries in just a fraction of the space.

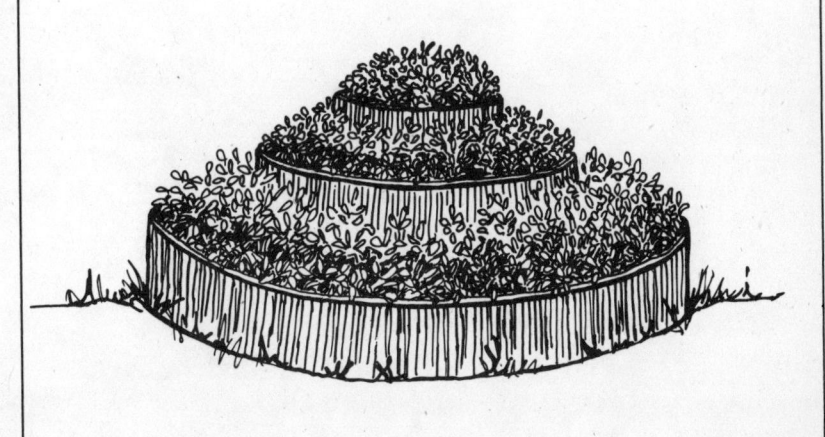

Finishing Touches 89

• • •

Furnishings. Outdoor furniture, like everything else, is a matter of taste—and there is no shortage of possibilities to choose from. You'll want a good solid table that doesn't wobble, an umbrella to provide some welcome shade, a set of chairs, perhaps a few lounge chairs. You might even want to consider installing a custom-designed awning at some time. But whatever your final choices, you'd do well to buy furnishings that are not only comfortable, but sturdy enough to stand up to the elements.

• • •

Fun and games. What summer is complete without a few lawn games like badminton or croquet? Or, if you have a cement patio (which, incidentally, makes an excellent dance floor on a warm summer evening), you might consider using a portion of it for shuffleboard.

—10—

TIPS FOR CONTINUED SUCCESS

Here are a few tips, tricks, and other miscellaneous wisdom that might prove helpful.

A Little Extra Gardening Know-How

Avoiding cold air. When you're laying out a new garden, it's helpful to remember that cold air acts like water—it flows down a slope and collects in low-lying areas. If you can, garden on high ground. If your garden is in a cold air pocket, these ideas can help:
- divert the flow of cold air with a hedge, low wall, or hay bales
- dig a ditch on the low side of the garden to drain off some cold air
- plant in raised beds; the lower lying paths between them act as drainage channels

Cross section of a raised bed garden.

• • •

Planning for drought. Conventional wisdom calls for locating your garden to receive maximum sunlight. In areas of little rainfall, locating the garden where part receives morning sun and afternoon shade will help to keep moisture in the soil. Placing the garden near buildings not only provides shade, but also protection from drying winds.

• • •

An extra boost. To provide vital magnesium for faster development of tomatoes, peppers, and eggplants, mix 2 tablespoons of Epsom salts with 1 gallon of water. Apply 1 pint to each plant just as blossoms begin.

• • •

Interesting combinations. Crushed eggshells mixed into the soil around cole crops provide the extra calcium that they need. Sprinkle coffee grounds over carrot plantings to repel the root maggot or around evergreens as an eye-pleasing mulch. Herbs prefer lime and gritty soil. If you live in an area where ground oyster shells are available, mix a handful into each planting hole for herbs.

• • •

Weeding smarts. Never weed after a rainstorm. Weeds left on moist ground will reroot quickly. Cultivate weeds early in the season: one hour of weeding in midspring is worth a full day in high summer. The best time to kill weeds is when they sprout.

• • •

Watering smarts. If you water frequently with a hose, drive double stakes of wood at every 10 feet or so throughout the garden to keep the hose from sweeping over the tops of plants and crushing them as you move from place to place. Avoid night watering; cool temperatures are conducive to the spread of disease. And did you know that a chrysanthemum in the garden is like a canary in a coal mine? The mum wilts before the other plants when water is needed, giving you an early warning to start watering.

• • •

Containing mint. The problem with mint is that it will push out of the garden and across your lawn if it's not kept in check. There are three ways to keep it in bounds: plant it in a large pot, put a deep edging around your mint bed, or sink a piece of chimney flue liner into the ground and plant your mint within its confines.

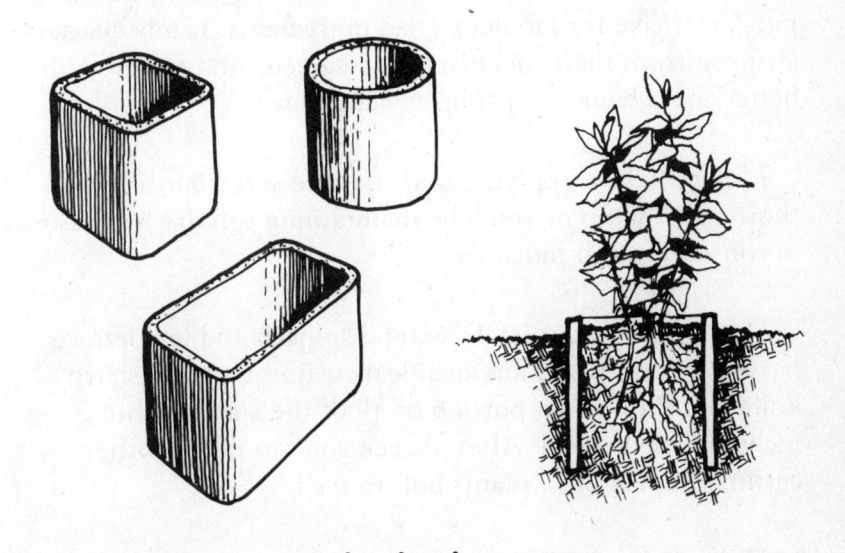

• • •

Let it dry! Stay out of a wet garden; diseases are easily spread when a gardener sweeps through a row of wet plants, particularly beans.

• • •

Harvesting smarts. Never twist eggplants or peppers off the mother plant. Cut or snip off with knife or shears, and leave a short stem on each fruit. Pick Patty Pan squash when they're no more than 3 inches across. Pick zucchini every day. Pick strawberries early in the day for best keeping. Place a flat stone under each cantaloupe to hasten ripening; turning is unnecessary. For earlier watermelons, pinch out blossoms after two or three fruits are set. Thump watermelons to test for ripeness; it should sound hollow. Look at the rind; it should be yellow where it touches the ground. Always cut (never pull) melons from the vine, and leave a short stem attached to the melon.

Tips for Continued Success 93

• • •

Squash seeds. Stick winter squash seeds in a partly finished compost pile. The squash plants will camouflage the pile, and receive plenty of nourishment at the same time.

• • •

Eat the weeds! Certain young weeds should be thought of as free vegetables. Dandelion greens and troublesome purslane make for fabulous salad ingredients. Lambsquarters, stripped from their tough stems, steamed, and tossed with butter, are a wonderful spinach substitute.

• • •

Mulch. Before applying mulch, make sure your soil is thoroughly damp or you'll be maintaining soil dryness instead of conserving soil moisture.

• • •

Don't pick it, cut it! To extend spinach and leaf lettuce harvests, don't pick individual leaves. Rather, use a sharp knife and cut down a portion or all of the stand within 2 inches of the ground. After a week you can take another cutting. Repeat until plants bolt to seed.

• • •

Multiple heads. For multiheads from a single cabbage plant, cut the main head, but leave the plant in the ground. In time, smaller heads will form. The same is true for broccoli. But, alas, cauliflower will only produce one head per plant.

• • •

Stagger your asparagus. To ensure a long season of asparagus harvest, plant the roots at varying depths. Shallow roots will send up shoots first; the deeper ones somewhat later.

• • •

Mystify the kids. Place a newly pollinated cucumber, still attached to the vine, into a small, narrow-necked bottle. As it grows, it will expand into the bottle cavity. When it has grown as large as it can, cut the stem, and see if anyone can guess how you managed to get the cuke inside!

• • •

More fun for the kids. Scratch the name of a child you know onto a young pumpkin. The letters will expand as the pumpkin grows, and will be quite large when the fruit is ripe. They make wonderful halloween gifts.

• • •

Good-sized garlic. For large garlic, plant cloves in the fall. They'll weather the winter perfectly, and continue making strong growth throughout the following spring and summer.

• • •

Onion lore. Onions have been used for centuries to treat a variety of ailments, including baldness, which supposedly responds to onion rubbed on bare spots while the patient sits in the sun. Onion juice was formerly sniffed to bring on sneezing and clear a stuffy head, or mixed with chicken fat to make a salve for blisters on the feet. And chopped onion soaked in honey was highly recommended as a cough syrup.

• • •

Learn to recognize "volunteers." Once you plant dill, you'll never have to plant it again. Let seeds from a few flower heads scatter each year. In the spring, be alert for the feathery green tufts that emerge everywhere, and save a few for transplanting when you cultivate.

• • •

Want to store carrots through winter? After digging carrots, let them lie in the sun for a couple of hours to dry well. Then cut off the tops, and put them in large plastic bags punched with holes. You can wash them or not. Keep them where it's cold, but not freezing, and they'll stay crisp for months.

• • •

Frost control. Hold back on nitrogen-rich fertilizer late in the season. Overly rich growth makes plants more susceptible to frost.

Tips For Good Maintenance

Clean your tools. Clean metal parts of spades, shovels, forks, rakes, and hoes with a wire brush or steel wool. Apply a protective coating of oil with an old cloth. Gently sandpaper rough spots on wooden handles and coat with floor wax.

• • •

In-season cleaning system. Fill an old pail with sand. Pour into it a quart or so of old motor oil and mix it in. After every use of your tools, push them into the oily sand a few times. They'll emerge shiny and covered with a film of oil that will keep them from rusting.

• • •

Tool rack. Attach an old rake head to the wall and use it as a hanger for hand tools.

• • •

Tool spotter. Paint a band of red, orange or yellow on the handles of all your tools. This will make them easier to find when you inadvertently leave one lying in the grass.

• • •

Fallen leaves. When autumn leaves fall, run the rotary mower over them before you rake to reduce their volume, and combat matting and blowing. Bag the shreddings and till them into your garden.

• • •

Fallow protection. Don't allow your garden to remain exposed to winter erosion. Mulch with shredded leaves or clean straw. Or better yet, plant a cover crop like annual rye that can be easily turned under in spring.

Miscellaneous Wisdom

Predicting rain. Before weather prediction became a science, gardeners had methods of their own for forecasting rain. Here are some the old-timers swear by (but don't plan a picnic around them!)
- morning sky looks dull red
- smoke drifts low to the ground
- sparks fly out from a campfire
- swallows fly low
- seagulls circle high in the sky
- bluejays come close to a building
- dogs and cats eat grass
- old folks' bones ache

• • •

Predicting frost. Here's a rule of thumb many gardeners use to predict overnight frost. If the temperature is down around 40°F by 7 P.M., it will most likely drop below freezing by morning. If a sudden frost catches you with your plants uncovered, you can save them by sprinkling them with cold water the following morning, but *before* the sun reaches the plants and the sudden change in temperature destroys the frozen tissues.

• • •

Getting help. Contact your nearest Cooperative Extension office for help with pest problems, soil tests, advice on canning, and much more. It can be a real adventure. The problem is that each telephone company has its own way of listing this service. The following are the most common:
- Cooperative Extension Service (look under "C")
- ———County, Cooperative Extension Service (or try "County Agent" or "Farm Advisor")
- U.S. Government, Agriculture Department, Cooperative Extension Service
- ———State University, College of Agriculture, Cooperative Extension Service

Mulch

Mulch is a layer of organic material or plastic spread on vegetable gardens and flower beds so that it surrounds the plants and shades the ground. An old and established part of the gardening routine, mulching in early summer is done for three essential reasons:

- It prevents weeds from growing around your plants by depriving weeds of sunlight.
- It holds moisture in the soil by reducing evaporation.
- It maintains the soil temperature at beneficial levels because it acts as insulation. Black plastic will also heat your soil for earlier planting in spring.

In northern climates it is beneficial to mulch your garden after the ground freezes to prevent erosion and the thawing and refreezing cycle that can heave perennial plantings out of the ground. Roots and bulbs can be exposed by this ground heaving and are likely to be killed by subsequent frosts. A protective mulch layer will keep your garden frozen, and this is best for your plants. Another option is to plant a cover crop late in the fall such as annual rye that can be easily turned under when spring arrives.

Mulch is distinct from compost (compost is mixed *with* the soil to improve its organic composition) because it is intended only as a top layer of insulation and protection. But over the course of summer organic mulch will decompose and can be worked into the soil as compost.

Before applying mulch, make sure your soil is thoroughly damp or you'll be maintaining soil dryness instead of conserving soil moisture.

Below are some common mulching materials. Experiment to see what works best for you and your garden.

sawdust	hay	polyethylene plastic
paper	shredded leaves	pine needles
wood chips	clean straw	pine branches
grass clippings	cardboard	coffee grounds

YOUR GARDENING NOTES